THIS IS A FIRST ENGLISH EDITION PUBLISHED IN 2018
BY FLYING EYE BOOKS, AN IMPRINT OF
NOBROW LTD. 27 WESTGATE STREET, LONDON E8 3RL.

PUBLISHED IN THE US BY NOBROW (US) INC.

PRINTED IN POLAND ON FSC® CERTIFIED PAPER.

ISBN: 978-1-910620-49-6

FSC www.fsc.org
MIX
Paper from
responsible sources
FSC® C001693

ORDER FROM WWW.NOBROW.NET

TOM HAUGOMAT

THROUGH A LIFE

NOBROW
LONDON | NEW YORK

DECEMBER 1955,
MUD BAY, KETCHIKAN, ALASKA

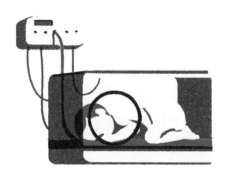

MARCH 1956,
PEACEHEALTH MEDICAL CENTER, KETCHIKAN, ALASKA

JANUARY 1957,
MUD BAY, KETCHIKAN, ALASKA

JUNE 1958,
MUD BAY, KETCHIKAN, ALASKA

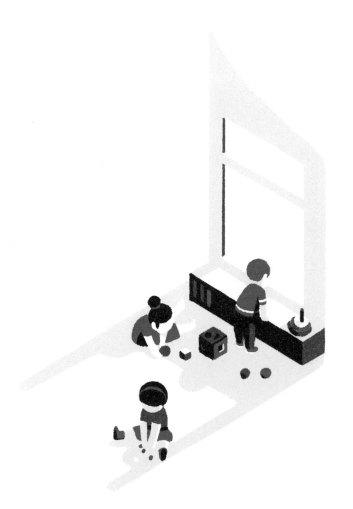

DECEMBER 1959,
CLOVER PASS KINDERGARTEN, KETCHIKAN, ALASKA

AUGUST 1960,
MUD BAY, KETCHIKAN, ALASKA

MARCH 1961,
PENNOCK ISLAND, KETCHIKAN, ALASKA

JUNE 1962,
MUD BAY, KETCHIKAN, ALASKA

DECEMBER 1963,
MUD BAY, KETCHIKAN, ALASKA

JULY 1964,
GRAVINA ISLAND, KETCHIKAN, ALASKA

MAY 1965,
PEACEHEALTH MEDICAL CENTER, KETCHIKAN, ALASKA

JULY 1966,
FAWN MOUNTAIN ELEMENTARY SCHOOL, KETCHIKAN, ALASKA

SEPTEMBER 1967,
MUD BAY, KETCHIKAN, ALASKA

MAY 1968,
MUD BAY, KETCHIKAN, ALASKA

JULY 1969,
MUD BAY, KETCHIKAN, ALASKA

JUNE 1970,
MUD BAY, KETCHIKAN, ALASKA

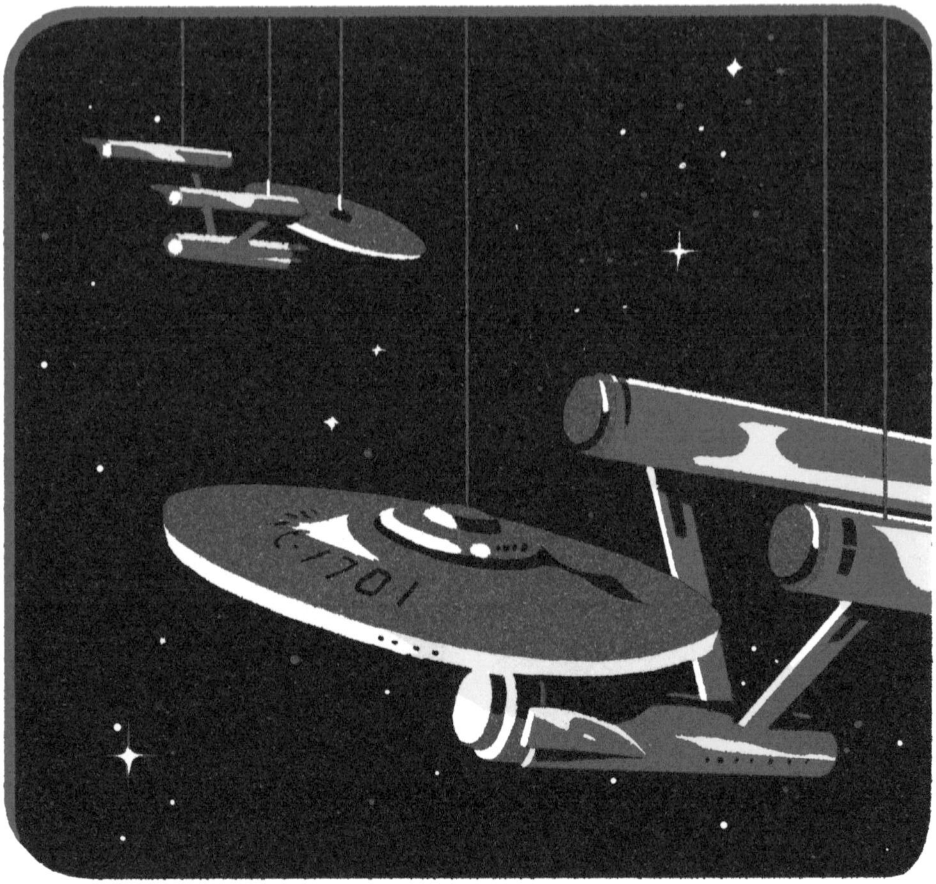
C-1701

JANUARY 1971,
PEACEHEALTH MEDICAL CENTER, KETCHIKAN, ALASKA

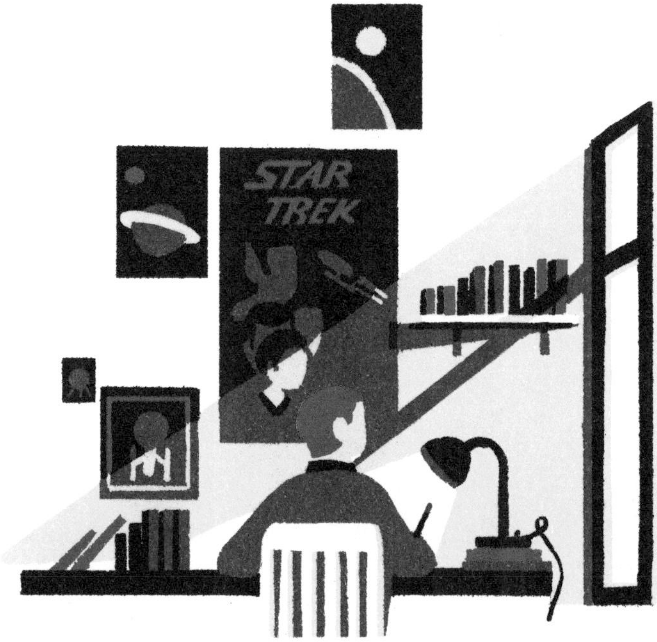
STAR
TREK

MAY 1972,

MUD BAY, KETCHIKAN, ALASKA

MARCH 1973,
MUD BAY, KETCHIKAN, ALASKA

SEPTEMBER 1974,
MUD BAY, KETCHIKAN, ALASKA

JULY 1975,
MUD BAY, KETCHIKAN, ALASKA

SEPTEMBER 1976,
MUD BAY, KETCHIKAN, ALASKA

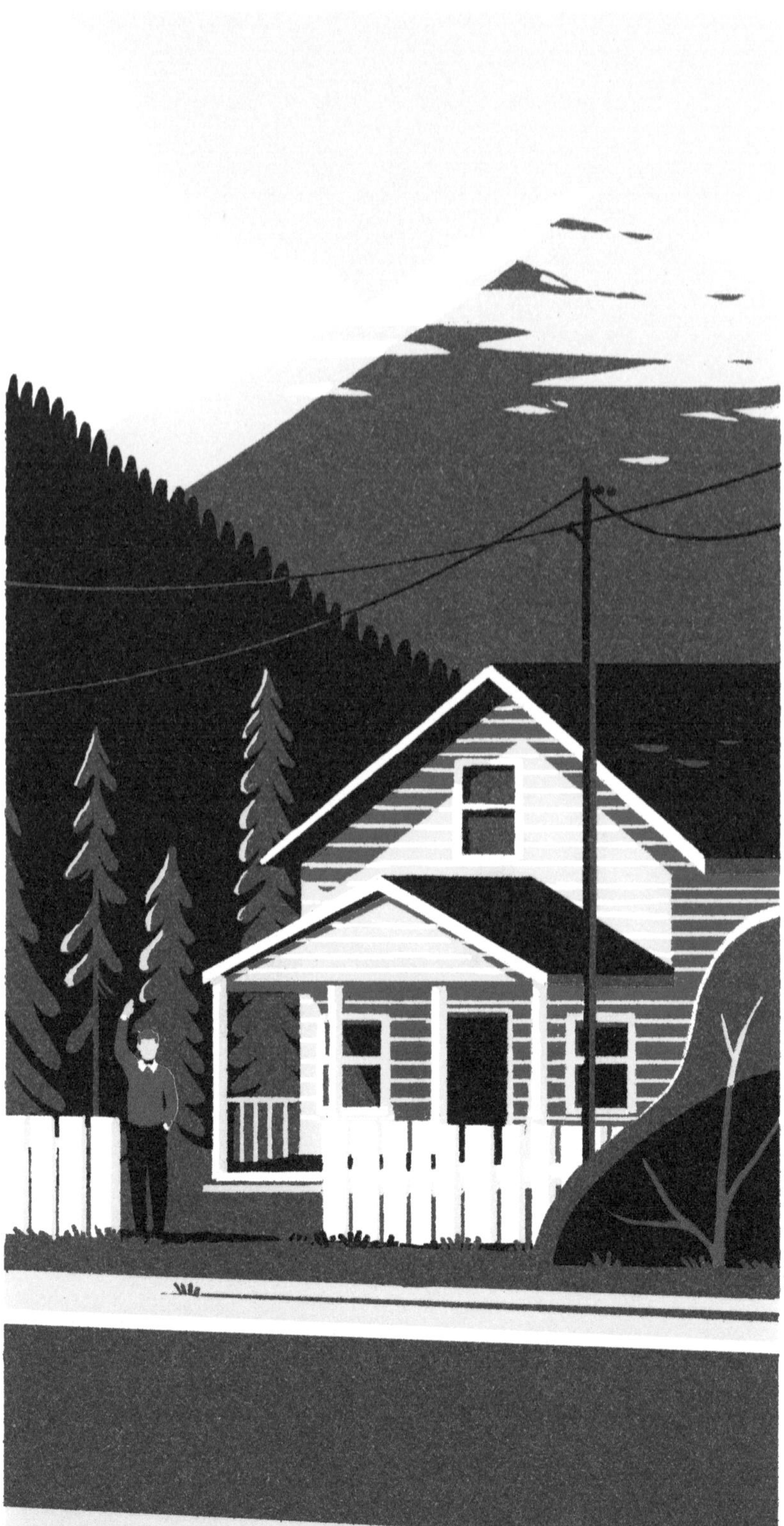

JANUARY 1977,
UNIVERSITY OF ALASKA, ANCHORAGE, ALASKA

Tiros-8

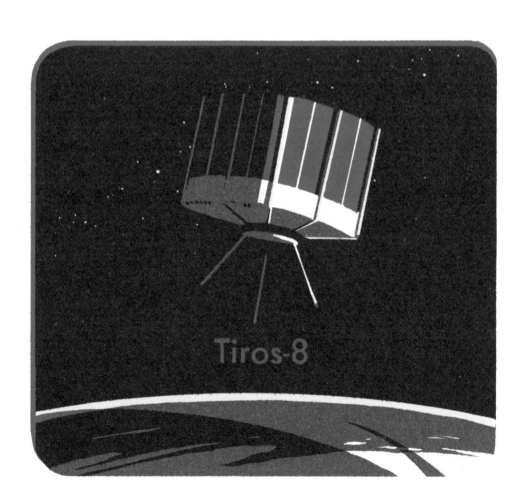

SEPTEMBER 1978,
UNIVERSITY OF ALASKA, ANCHORAGE, ALASKA

MAY 1979,
FOURTH AVENUE THEATRE, ANCHORAGE, ALASKA

JULY 1980,
CAMPBELL LAKE, ANCHORAGE, ALASKA

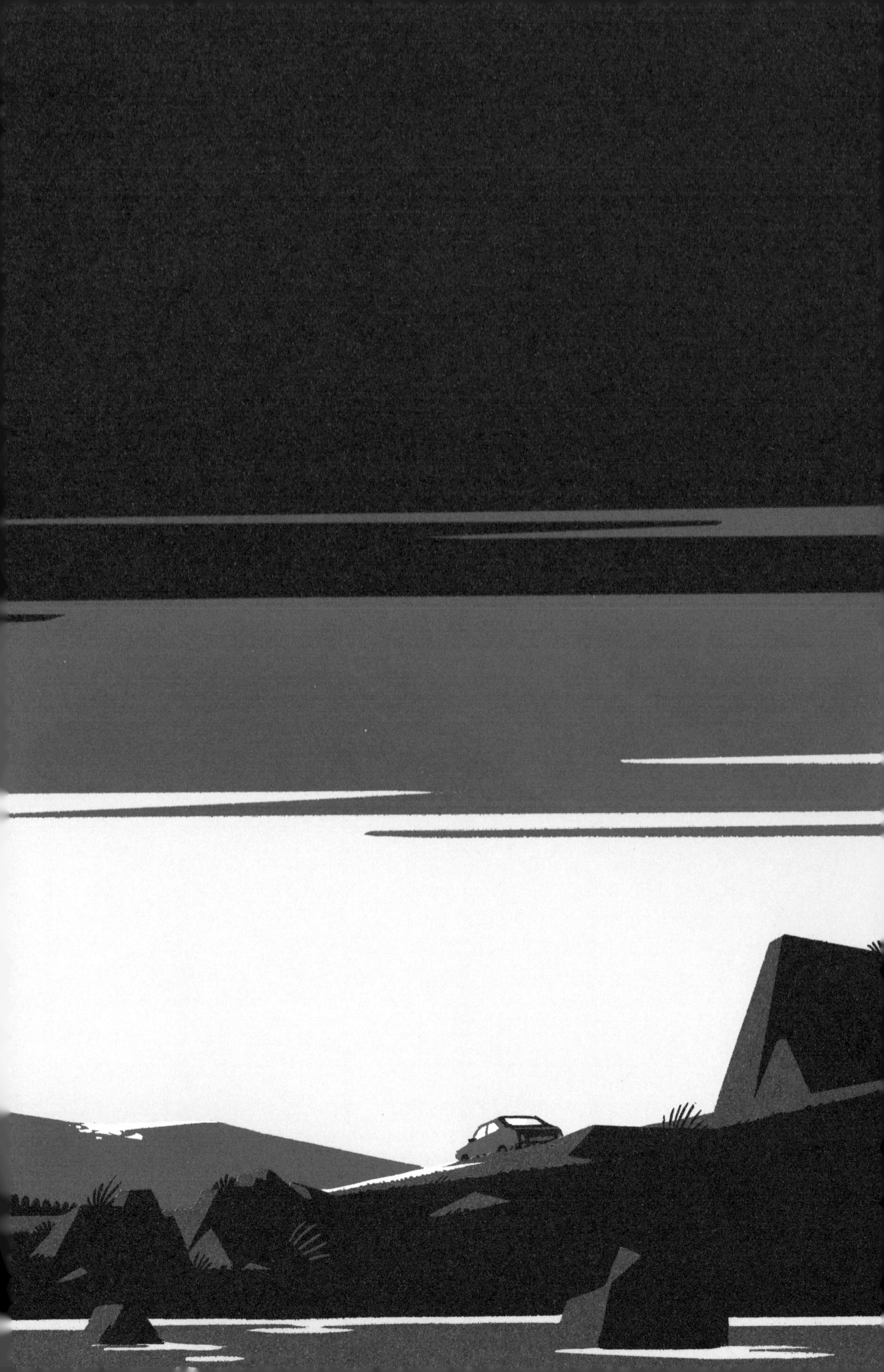

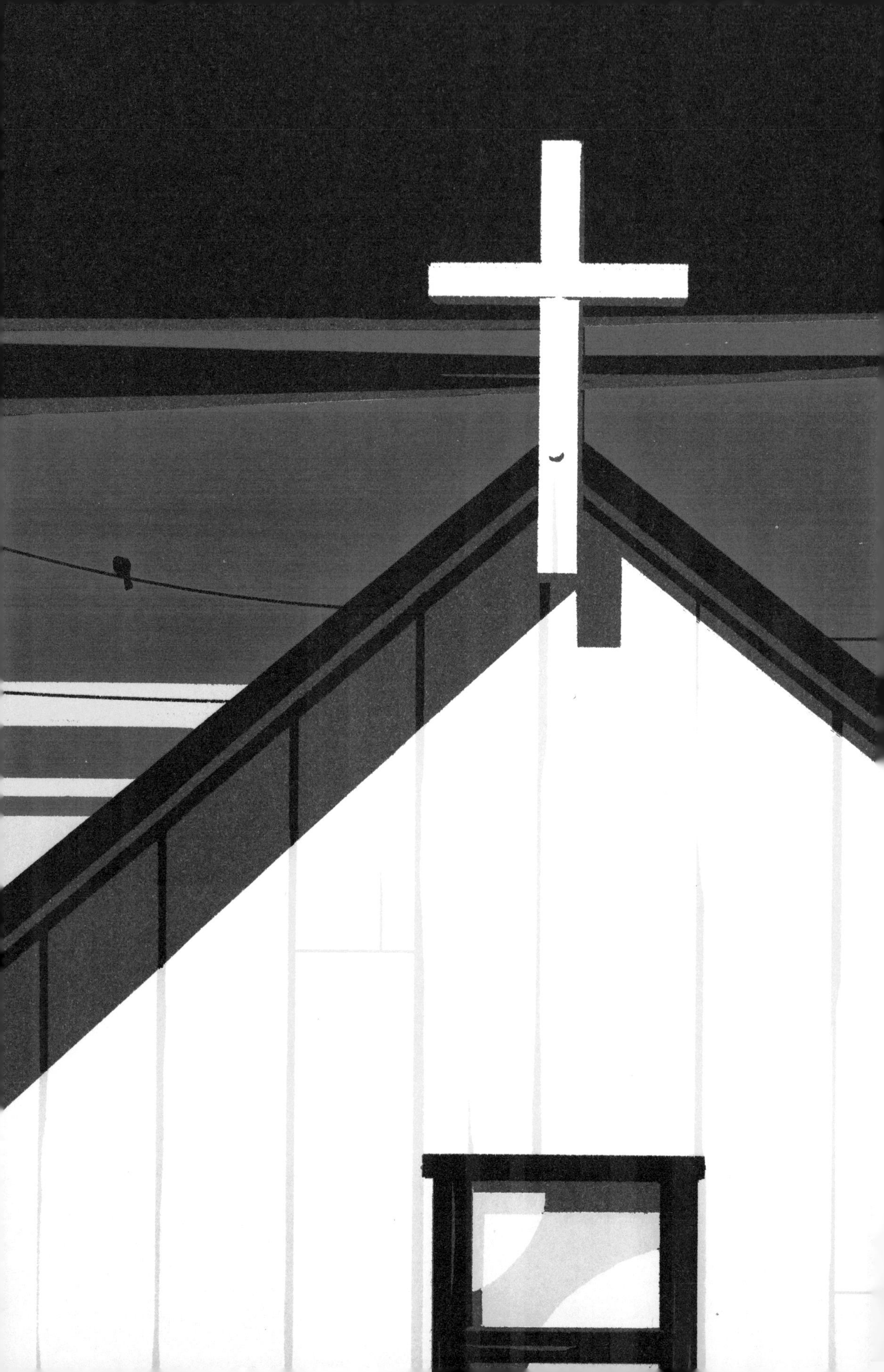

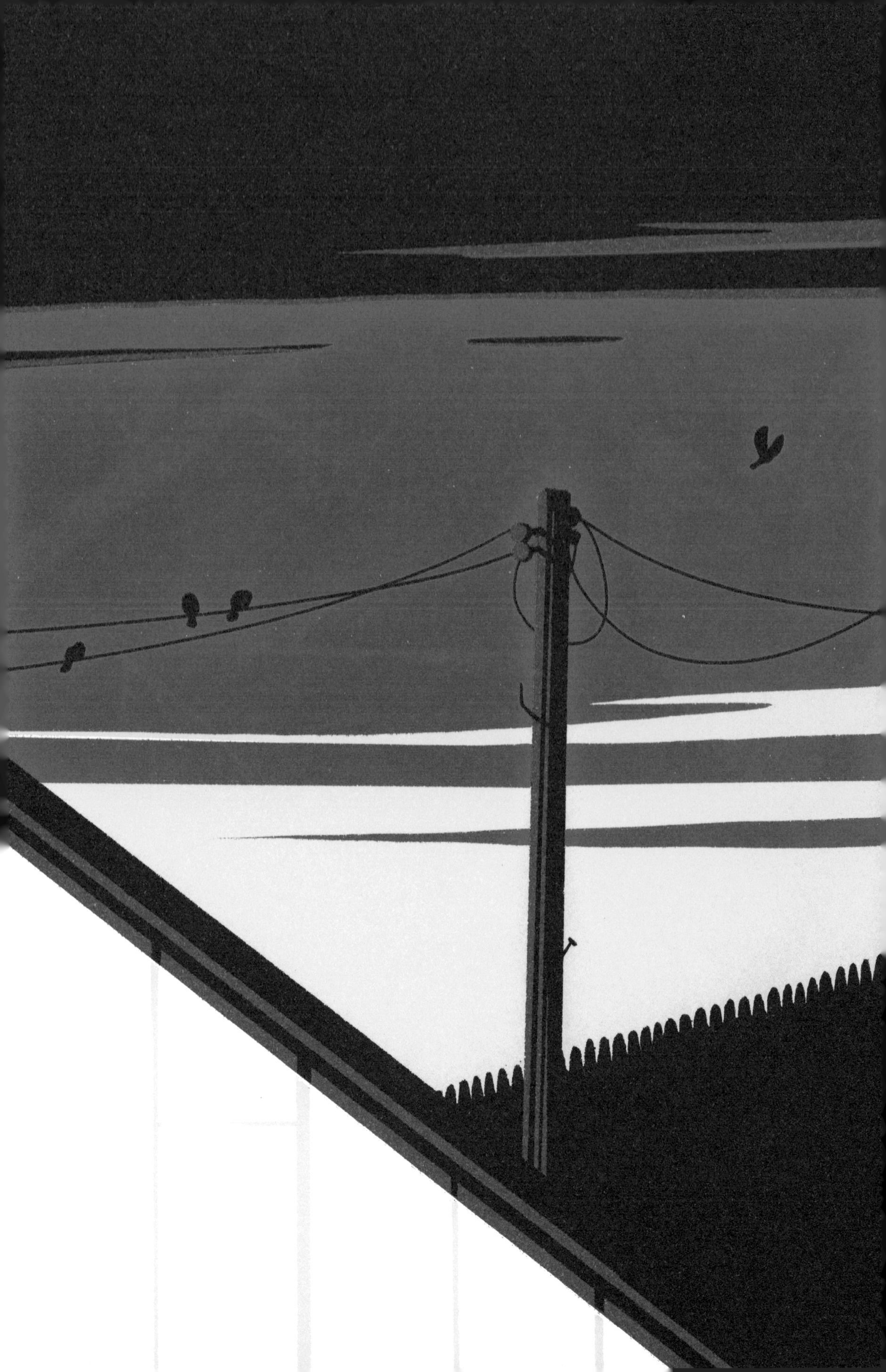

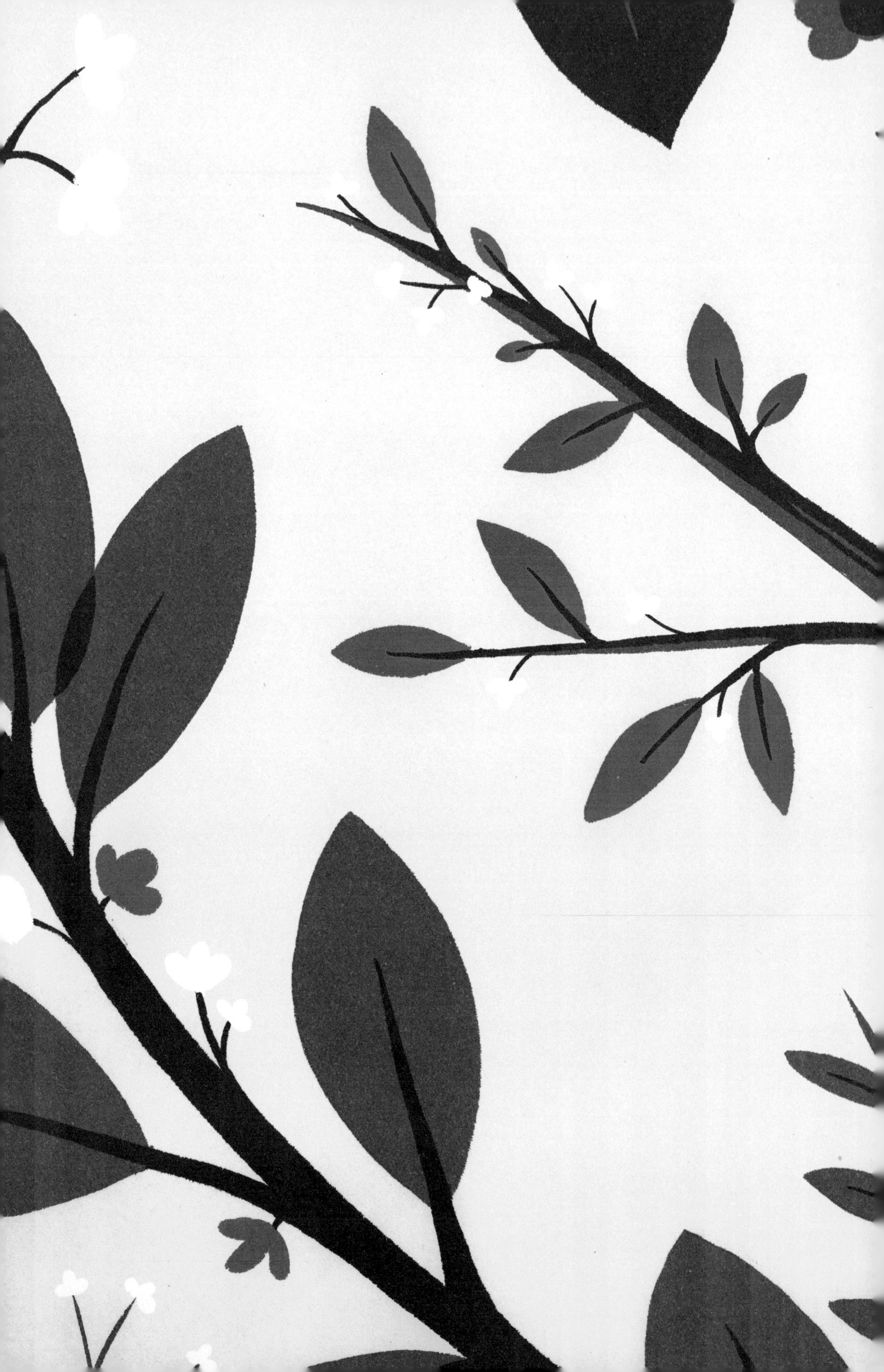

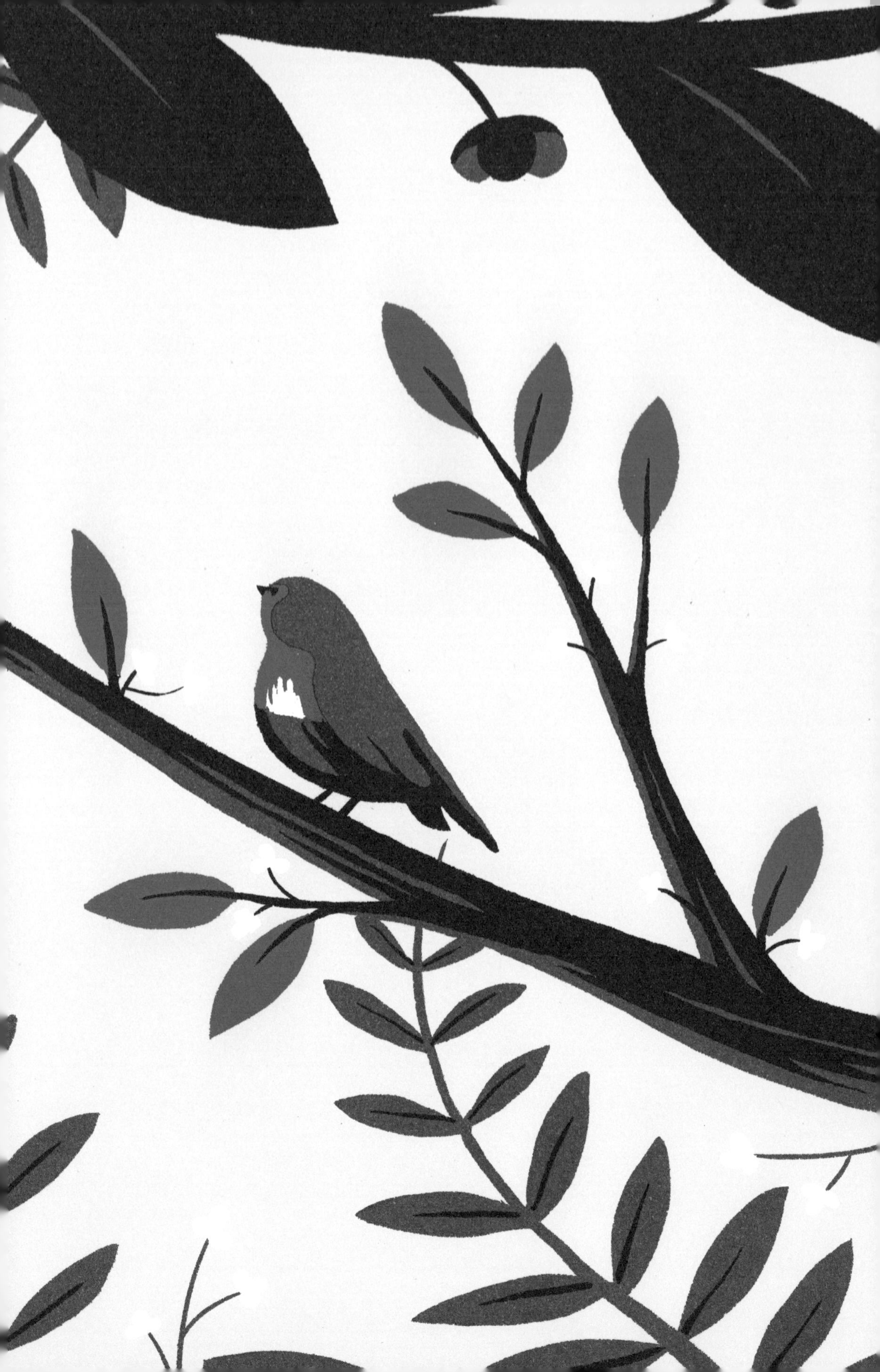

MAY 1981,
GRAVINA ISLAND CHURCH, KETCHIKAN, ALASKA

DECEMBER 1982,
PENNOCK ISLAND, KETCHIKAN, ALASKA

SEPTEMBER 1983,
SABINE STREET, HOUSTON, TEXAS

JANUARY 1984,
JOHNSON SPACE CENTER, HOUSTON, TEXAS

,TRATION
CENTER

NASA

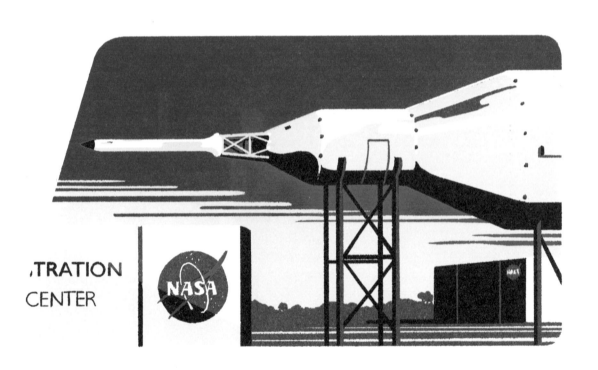

JULY 1985,
JOHNSON SPACE CENTER, HOUSTON, TEXAS

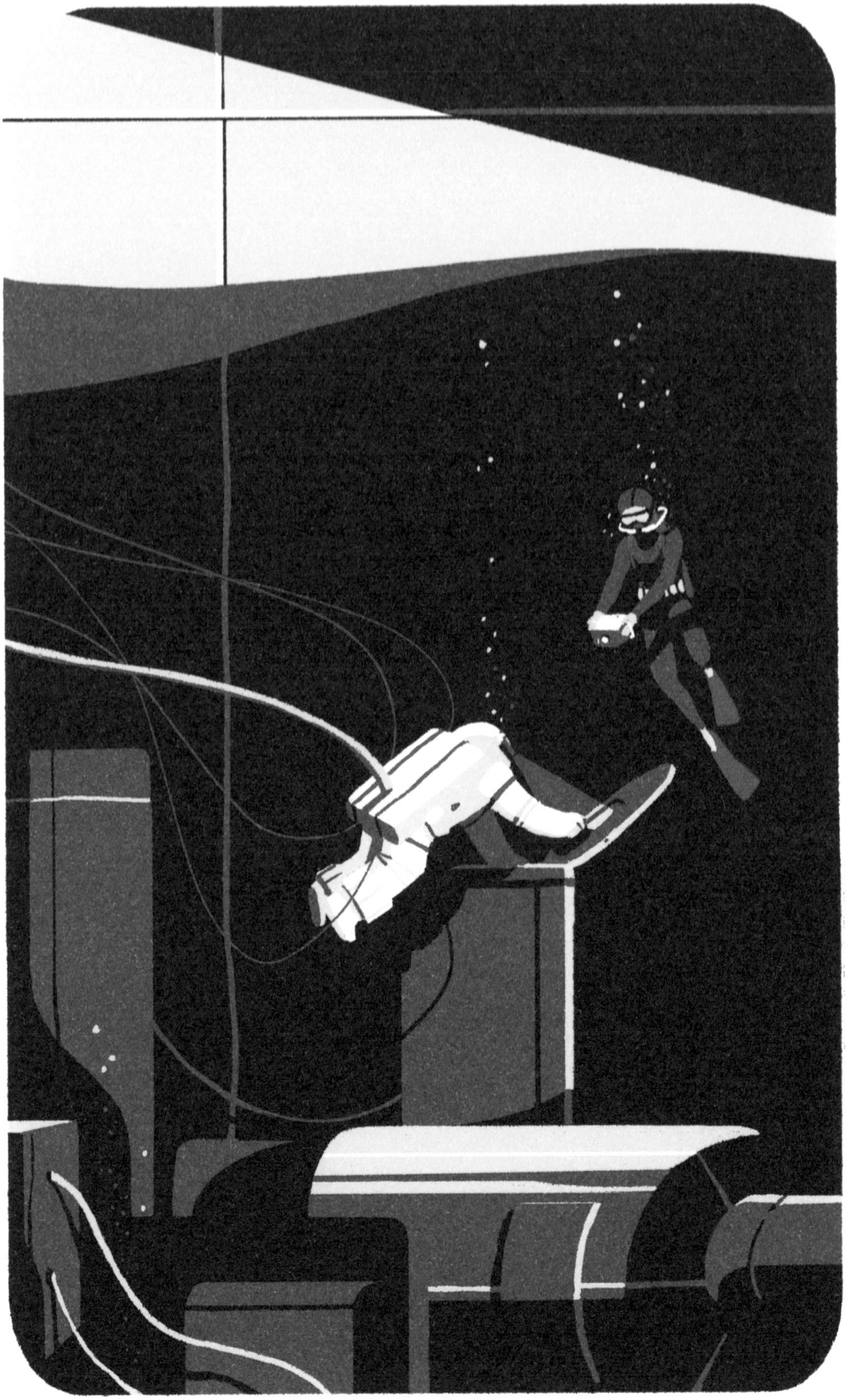

JANUARY 1986,
JOHNSON SPACE CENTER, HOUSTON, TEXAS

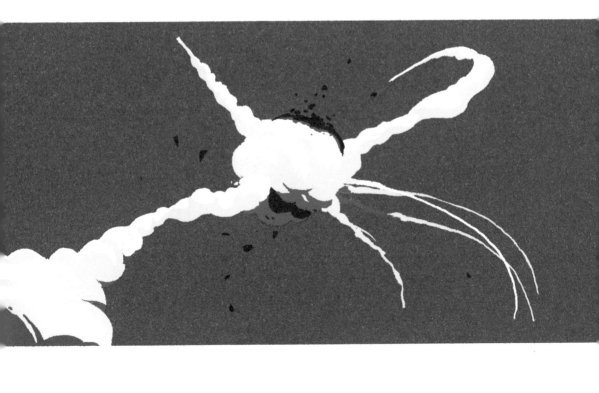

AUGUST 1987,
JOHNSON SPACE CENTER, HOUSTON, TEXAS

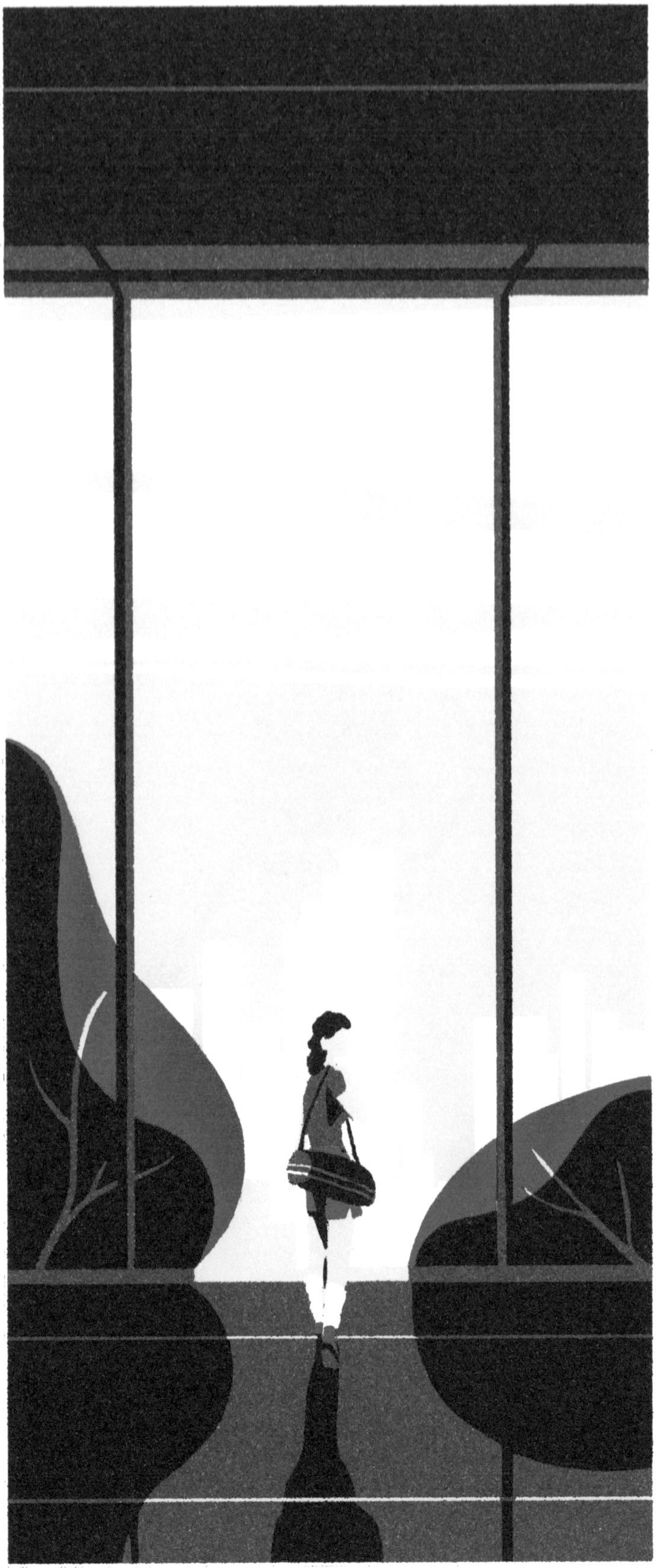

DECEMBER 1988,
JOHNSON SPACE CENTER, HOUSTON, TEXAS

APRIL 1989,
HOUSTON ZOO, HOUSTON, TEXAS

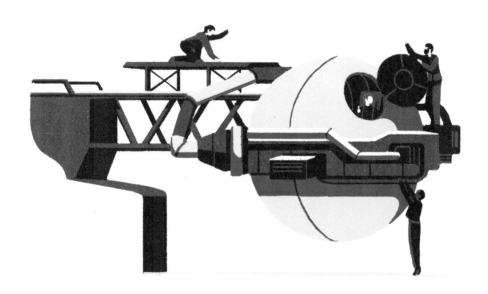

JANUARY 1990,
JOHNSON SPACE CENTER, HOUSTON, TEXAS

APRIL 1990,
SHUTTLE DISCOVERY, KENNEDY SPACE CENTER, CAPE CANAVERAL, FLORID

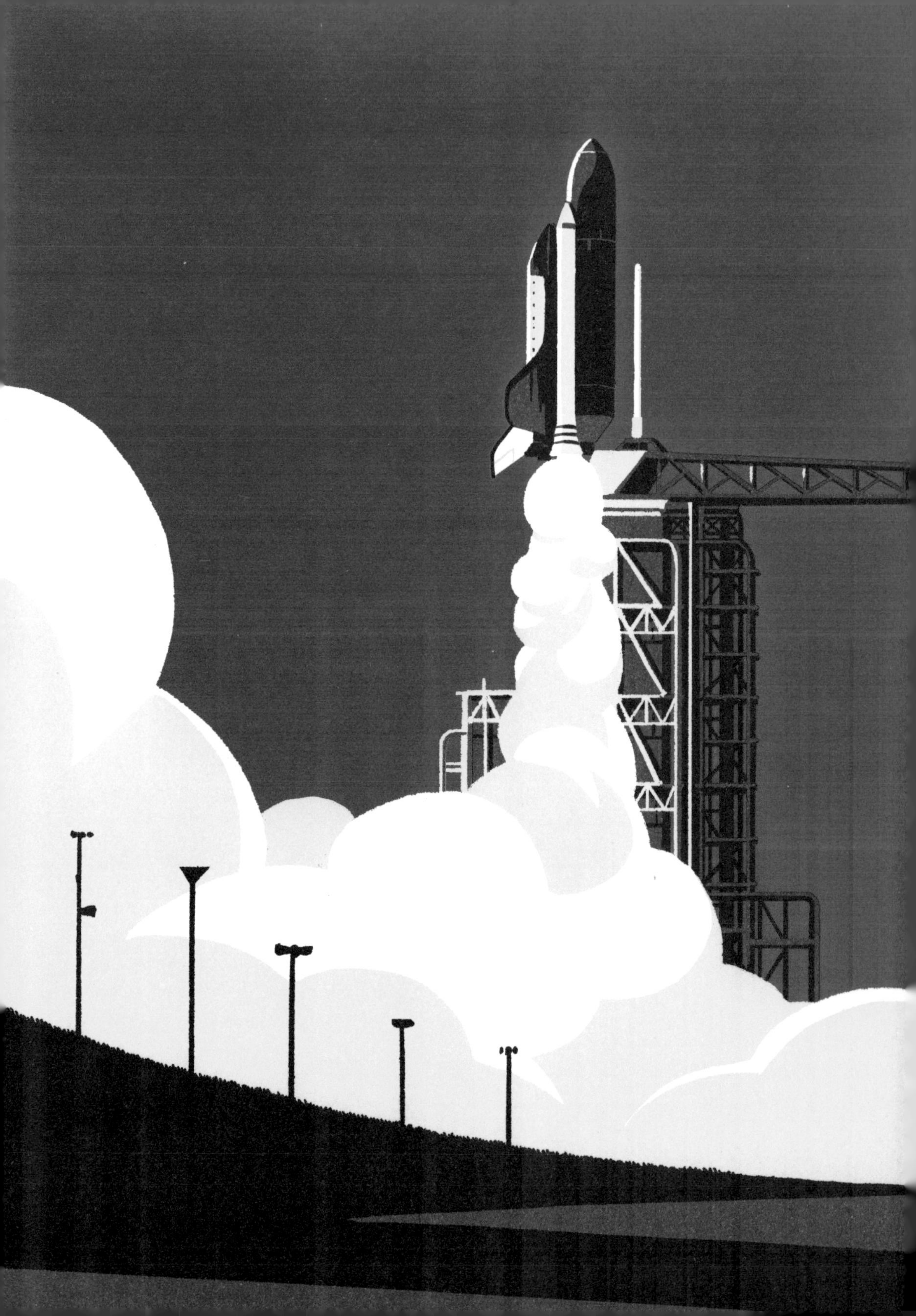

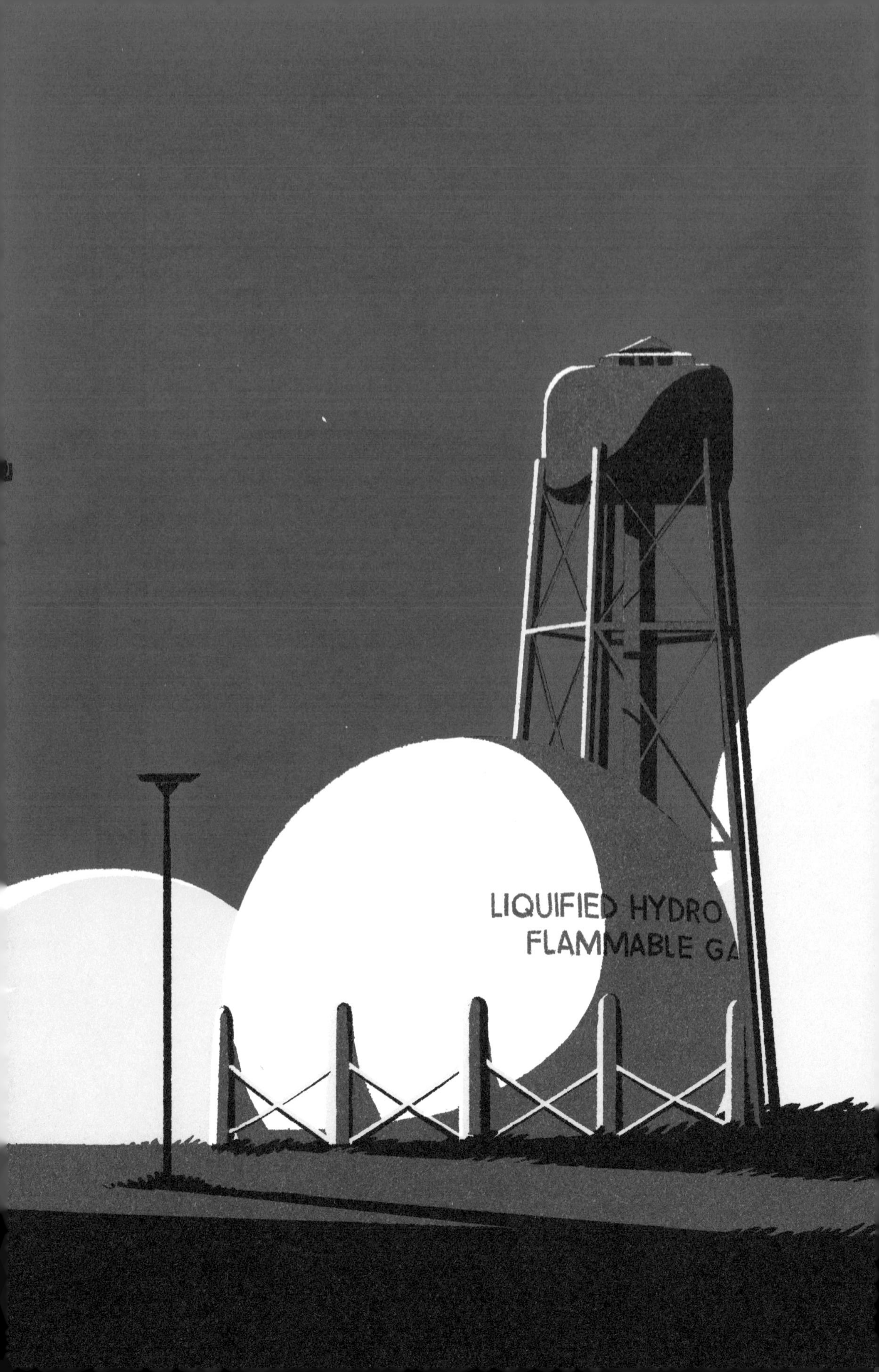
LIQUIFIED HYDRO
FLAMMABLE GA

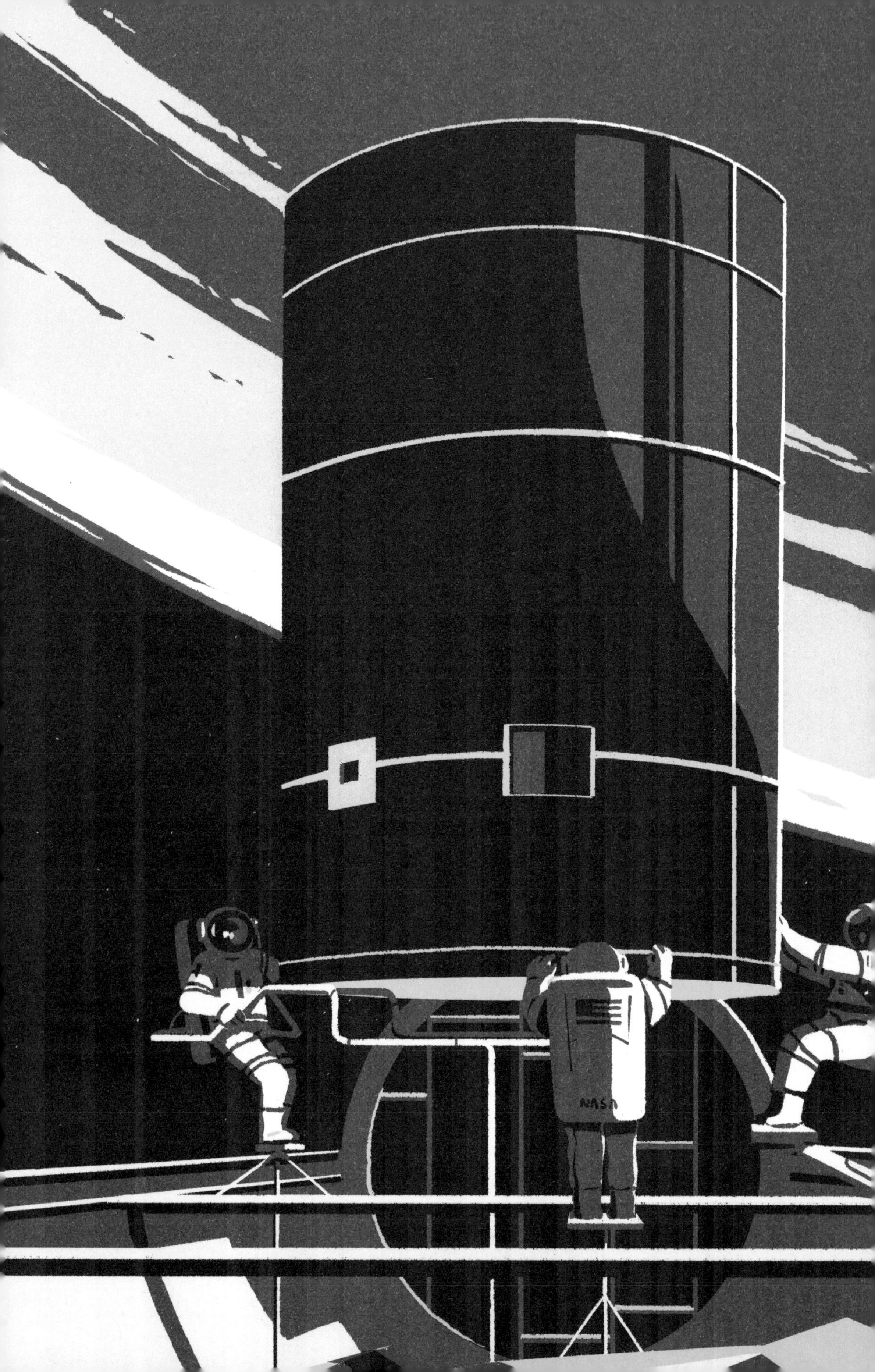
NASA

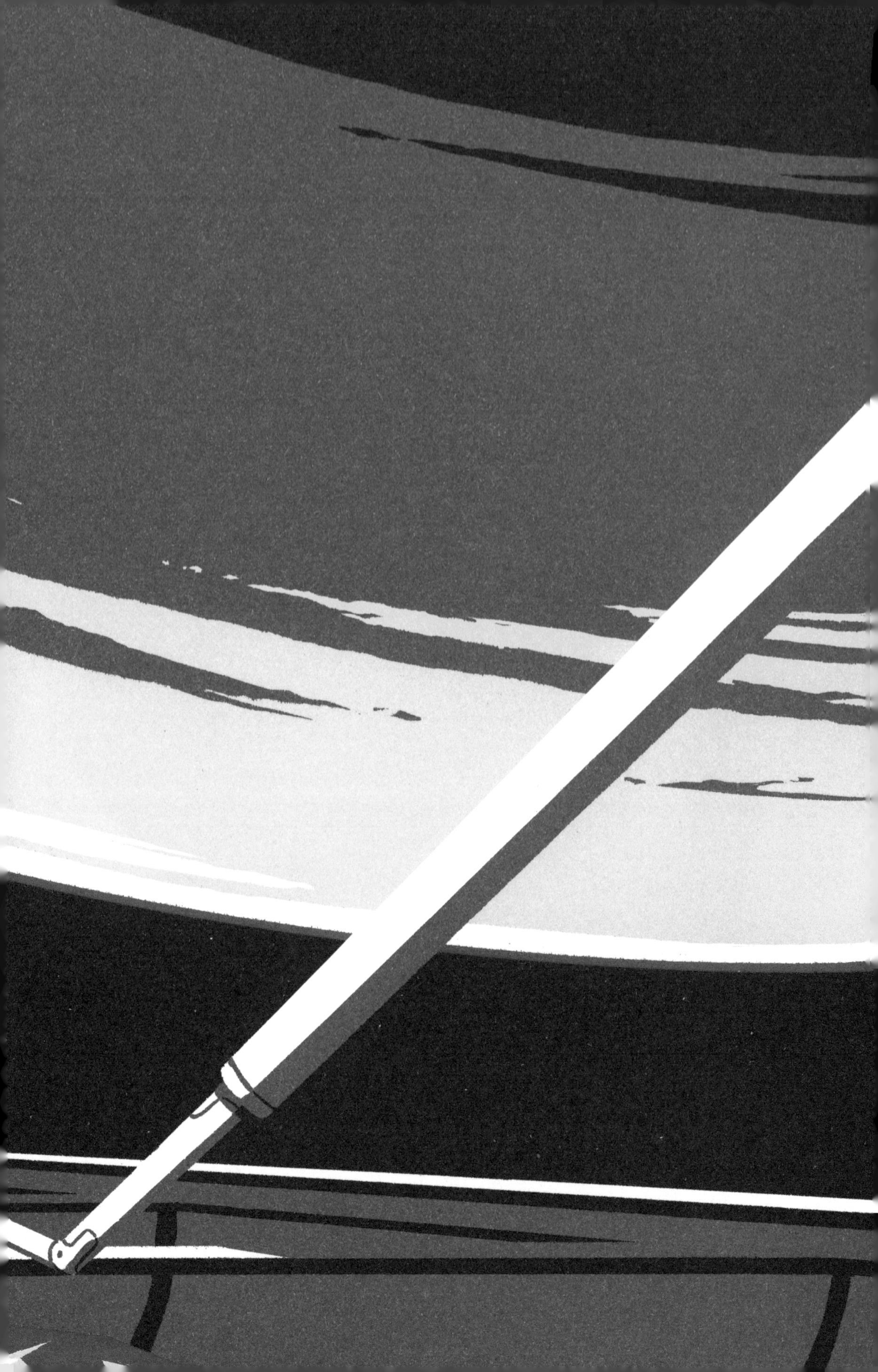

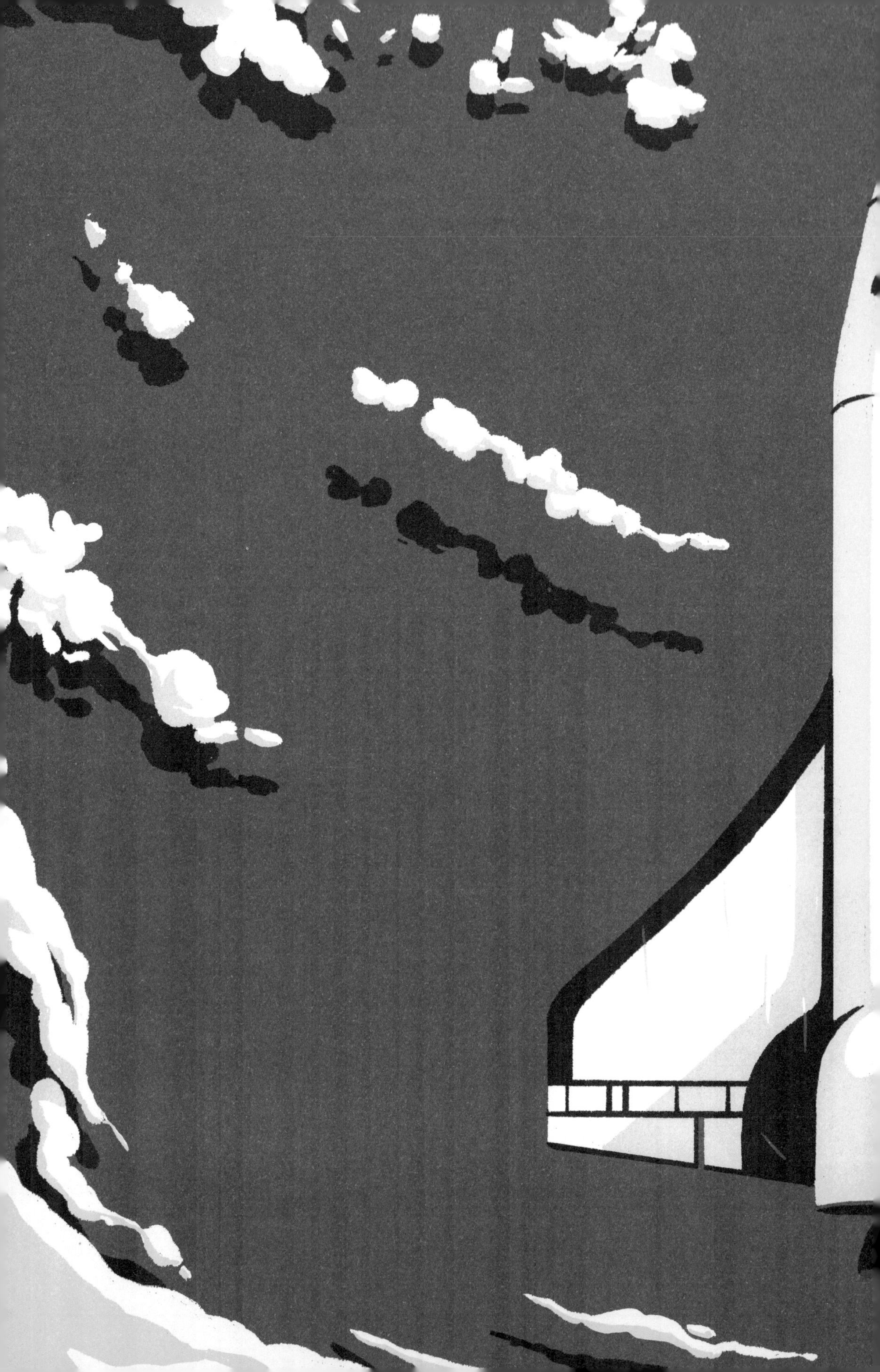

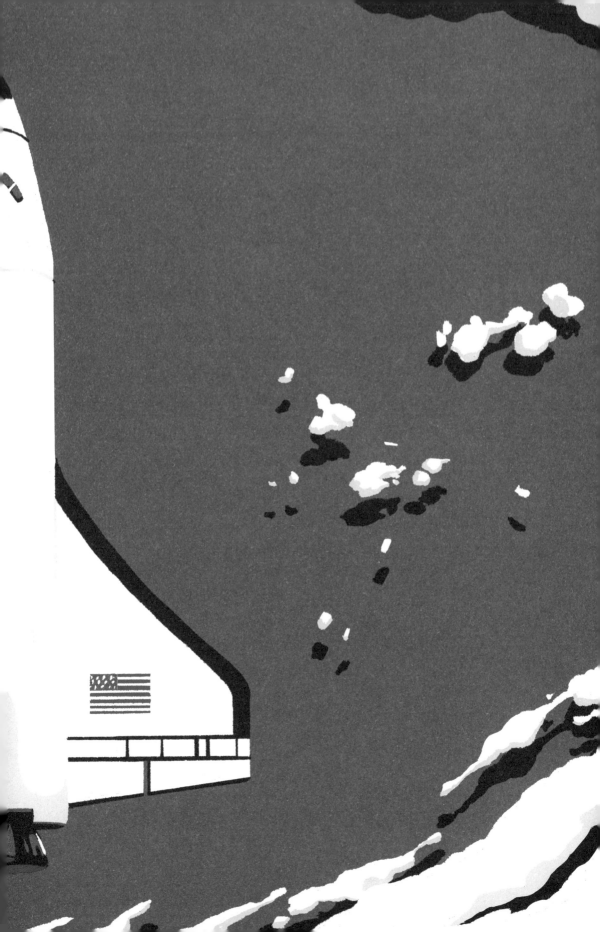

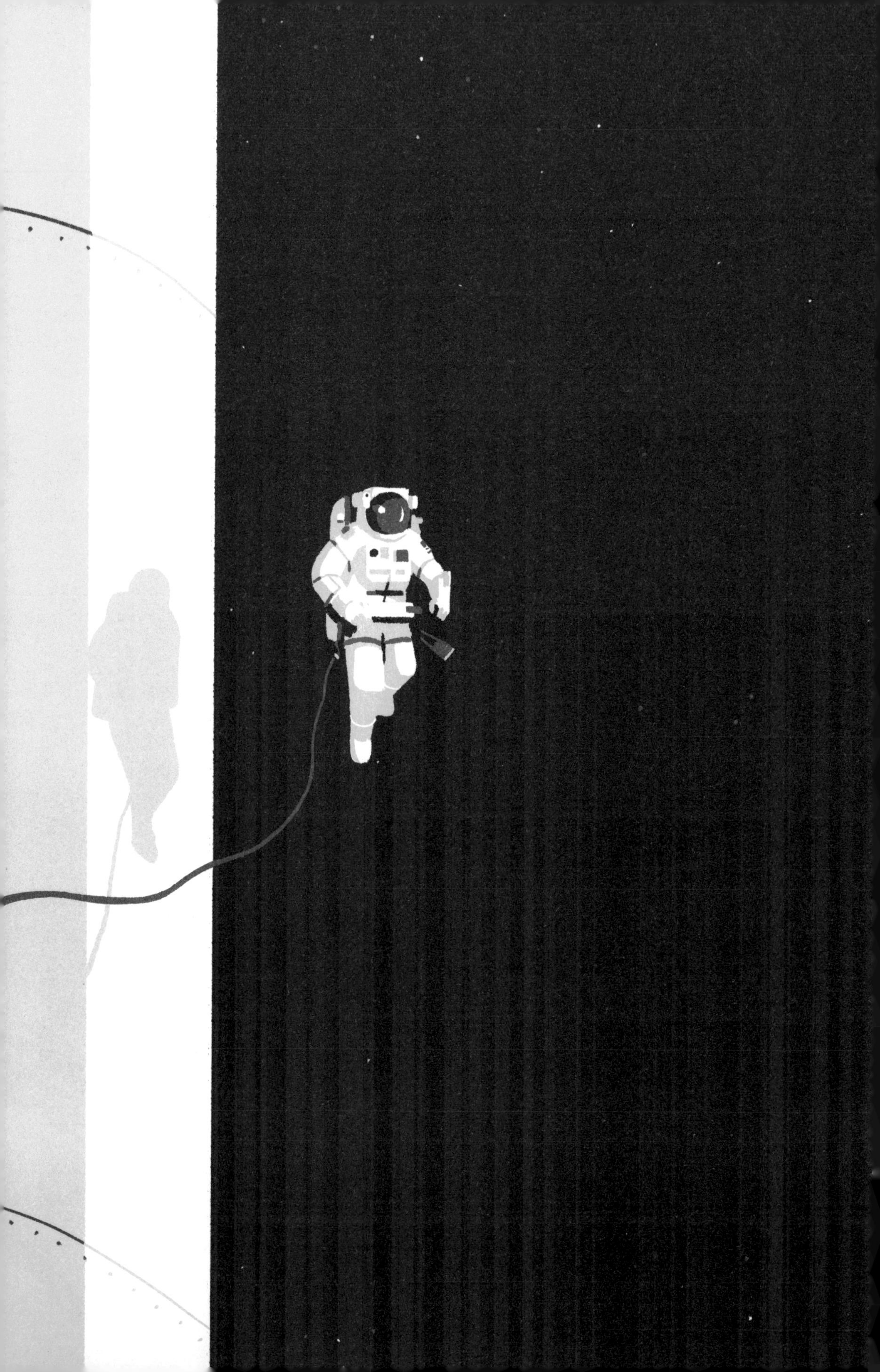

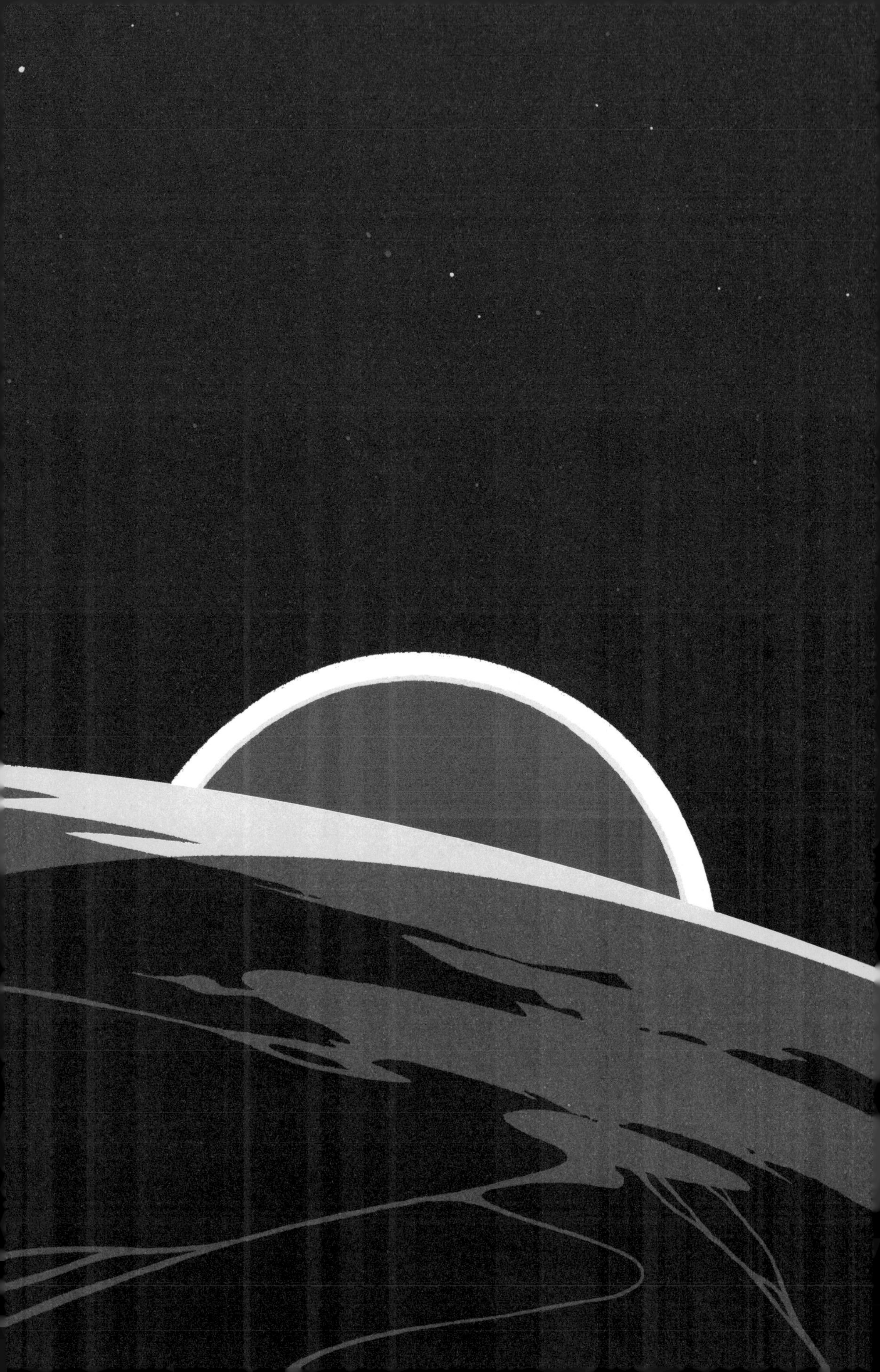

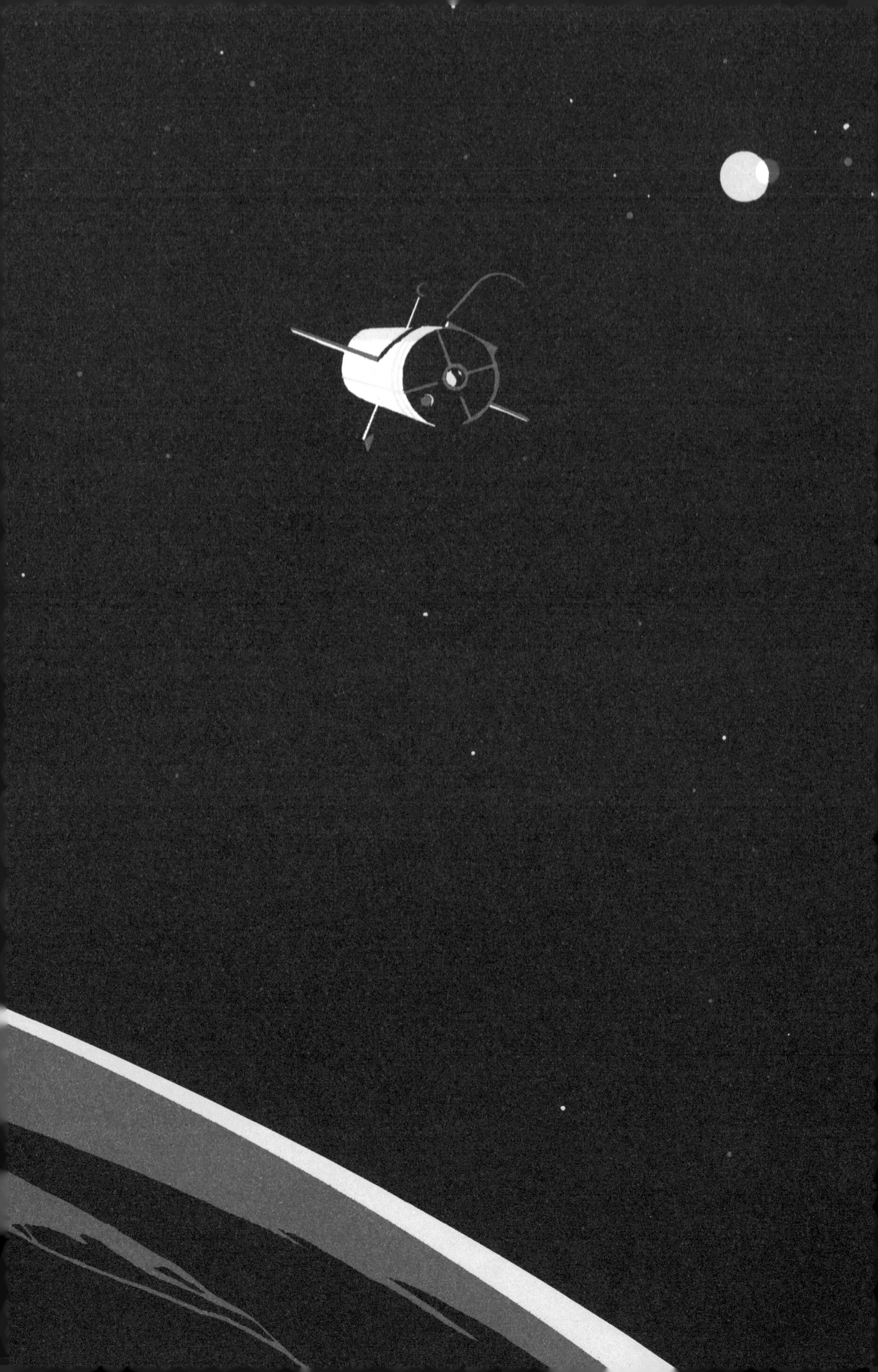

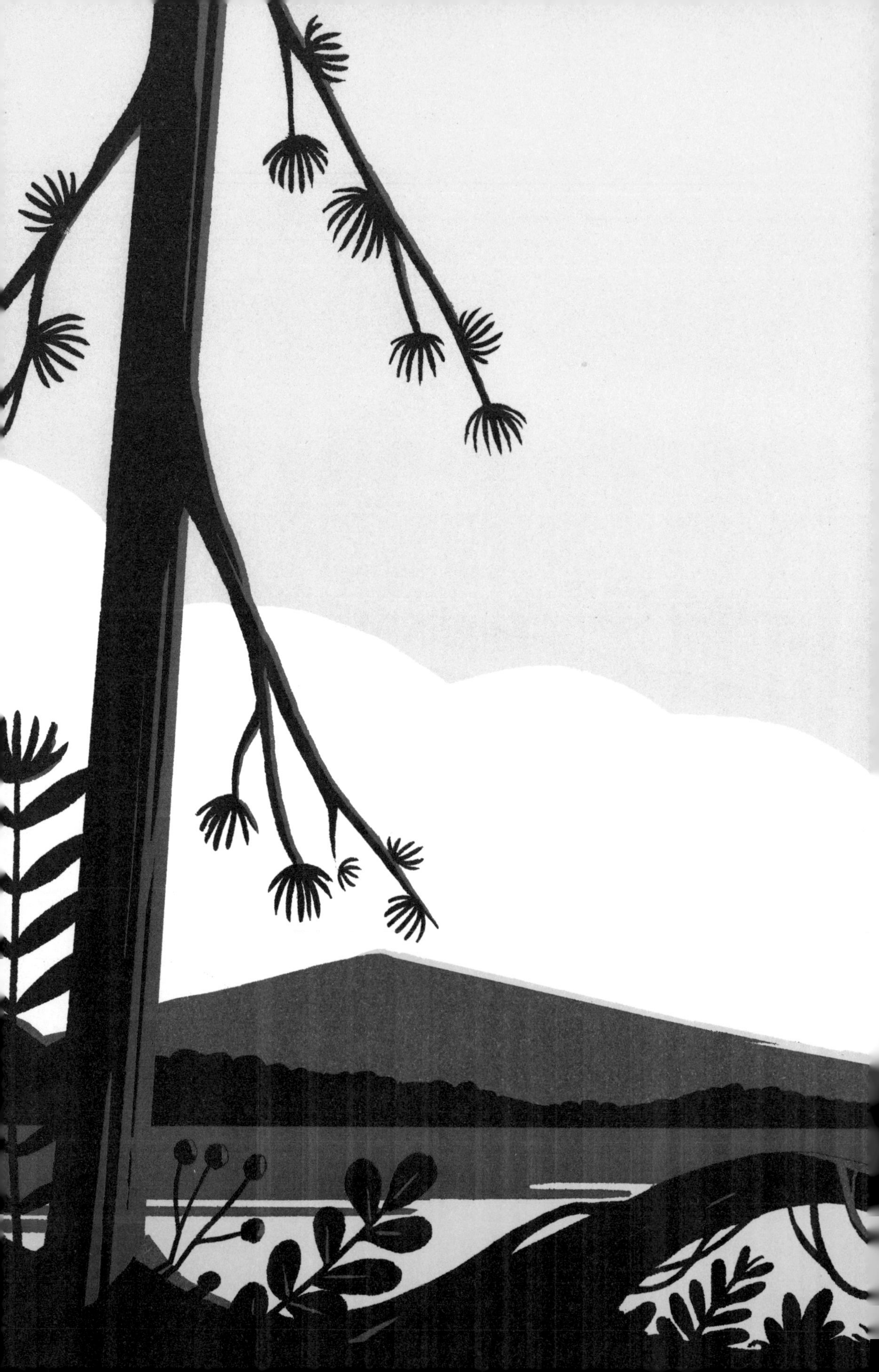

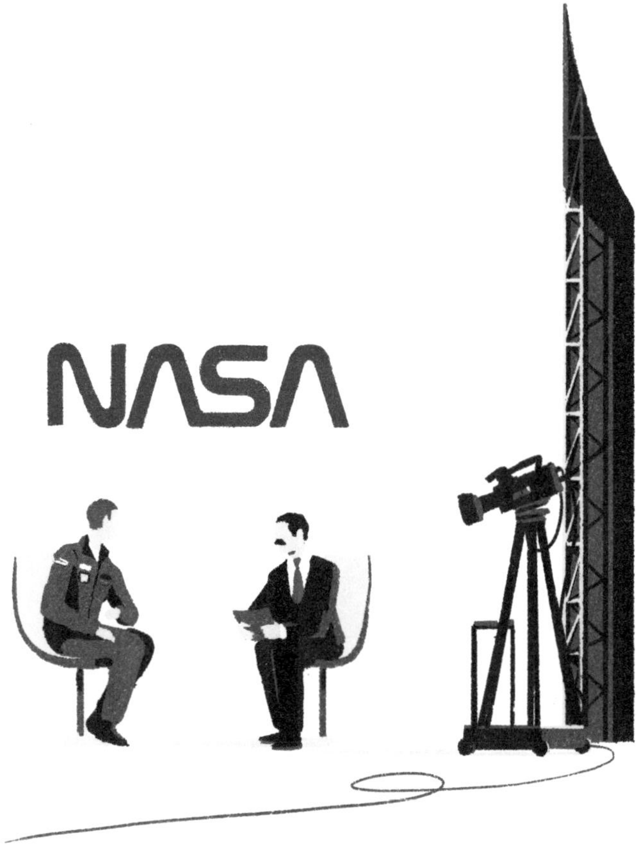
NASA

JANUARY 1992,
ABC NEWS, HOUSTON, TEXAS

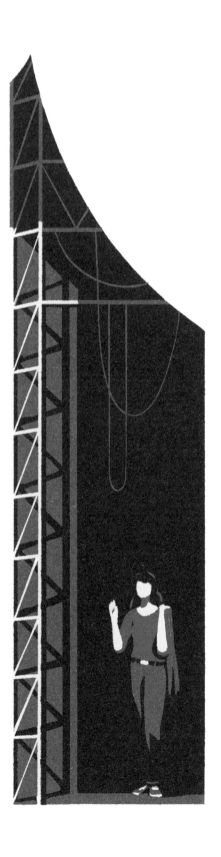

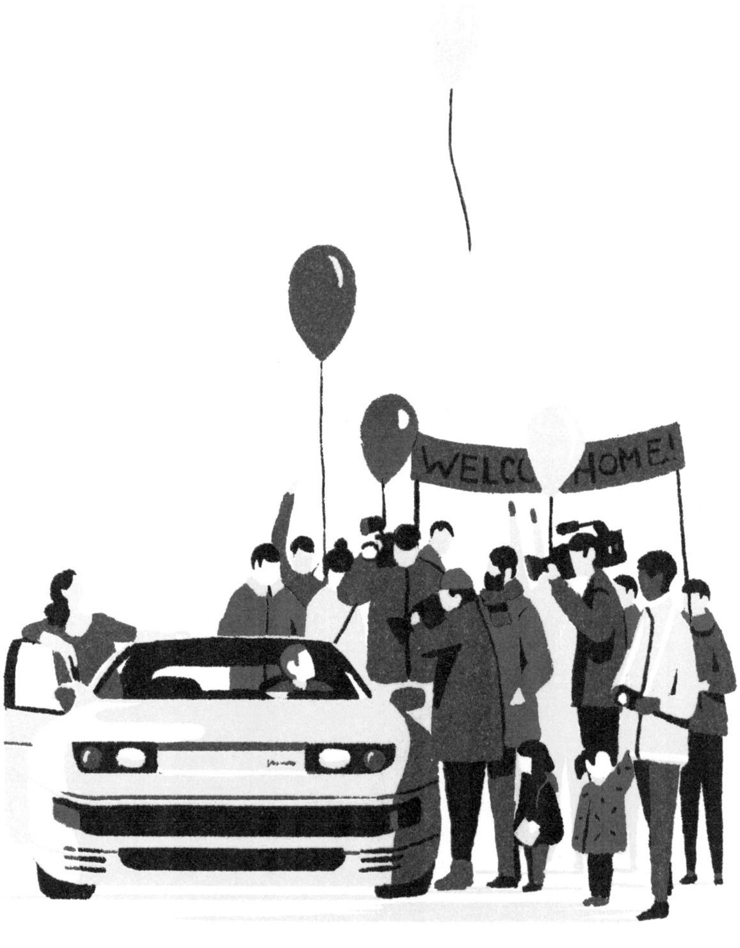
WELCO
HOME!

JUNE 1993,
MUD BAY, KETCHIKAN, ALASKA

MARCH 1994,
CAPITOL STREET, HOUSTON, TEXAS

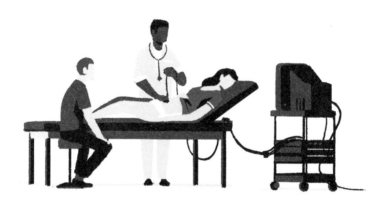

NOVEMBER 1995
ST. JOSEPH MEDICAL CENTER, HOUSTON, TEXAS

1995
20 NOV
15:55

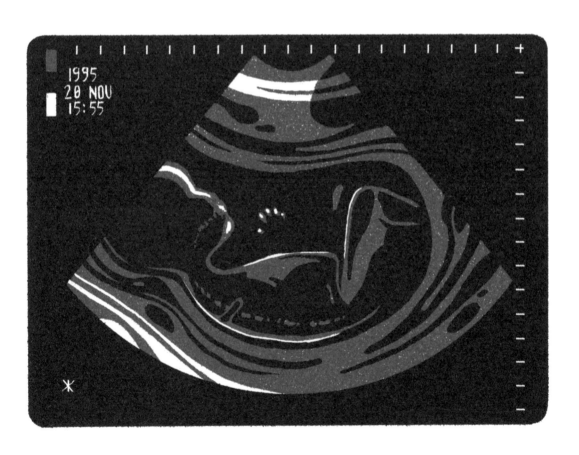

JUNE 1996,
CAPITOL STREET, HOUSTON, TEXAS

NOVEMBER 1997,
JOHNSON SPACE CENTER, HOUSTON, TEXAS

MAY 1998,
CAPITOL STREET, HOUSTON, TEXAS

DECEMBER 1999,
CAPITOL STREET, HOUSTON, TEXAS

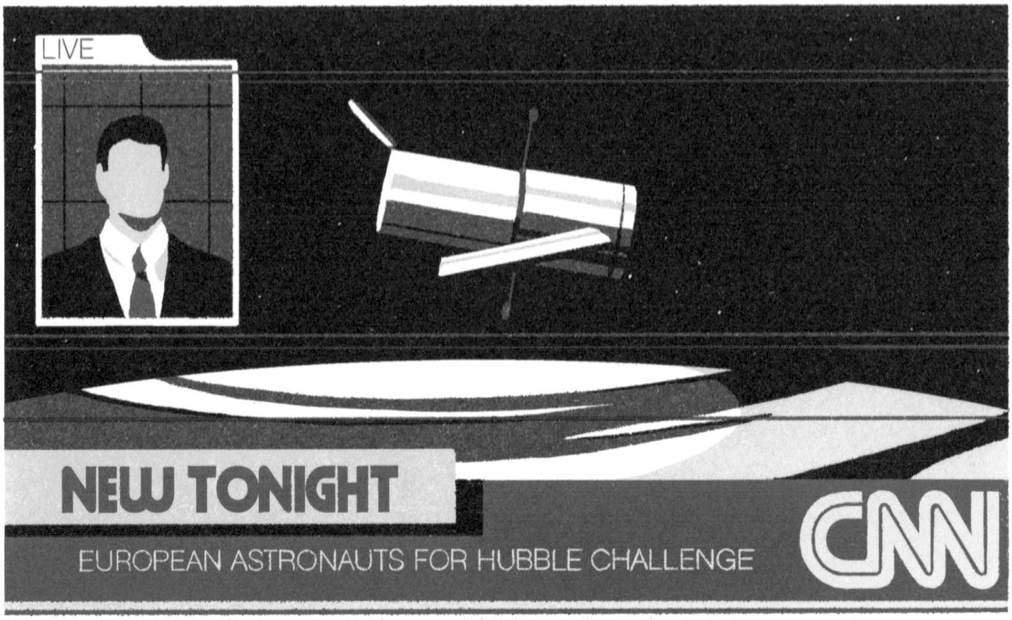
LIVE
NEW TONIGHT
EUROPEAN ASTRONAUTS FOR HUBBLE CHALLENGE
CNN

MARCH 2000,
JOHNSON SPACE CENTER, HOUSTON, TEXAS

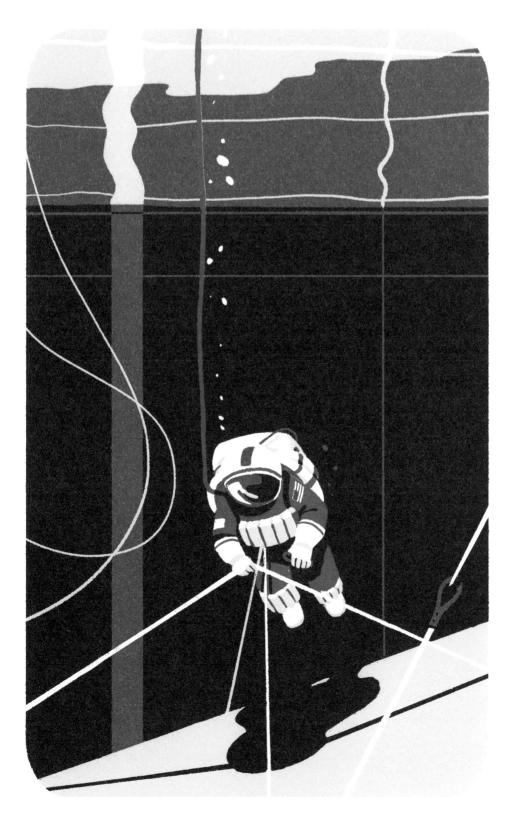

SEPTEMBER 2001,
SUNNY'S BAR, HOUSTON, TEXAS

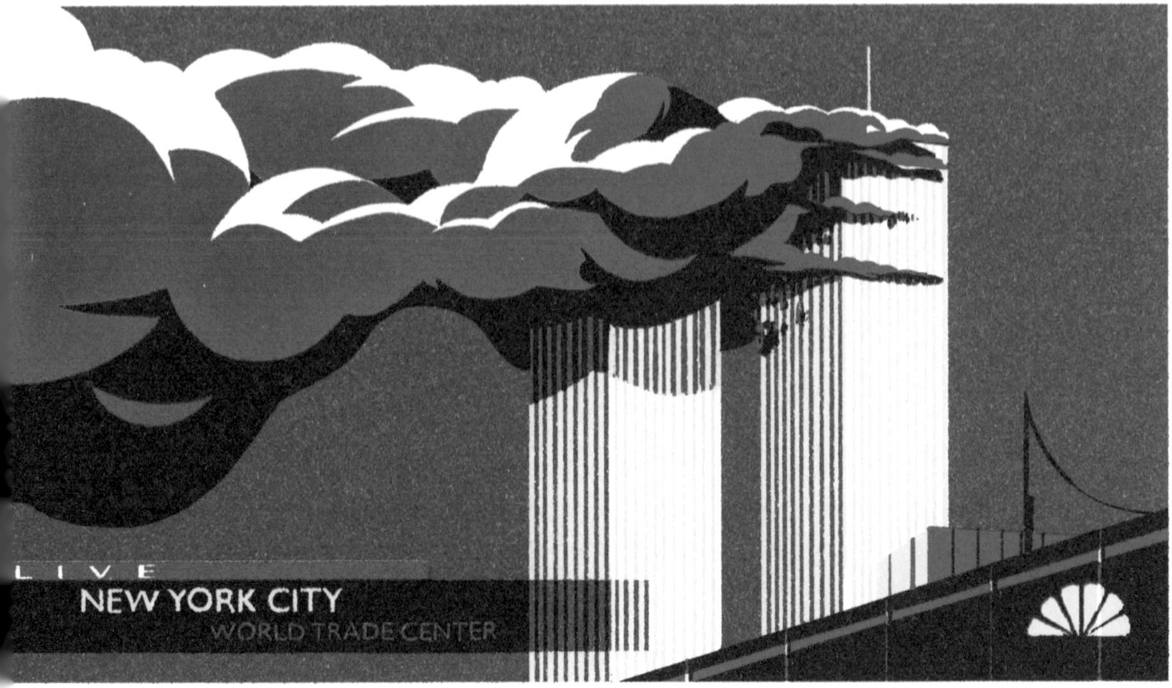
L I V E
NEW YORK CITY
WORLD TRADE CENTER

DECEMBER 2002,
JOHNSON SPACE CENTER, HOUSTON, TEXAS

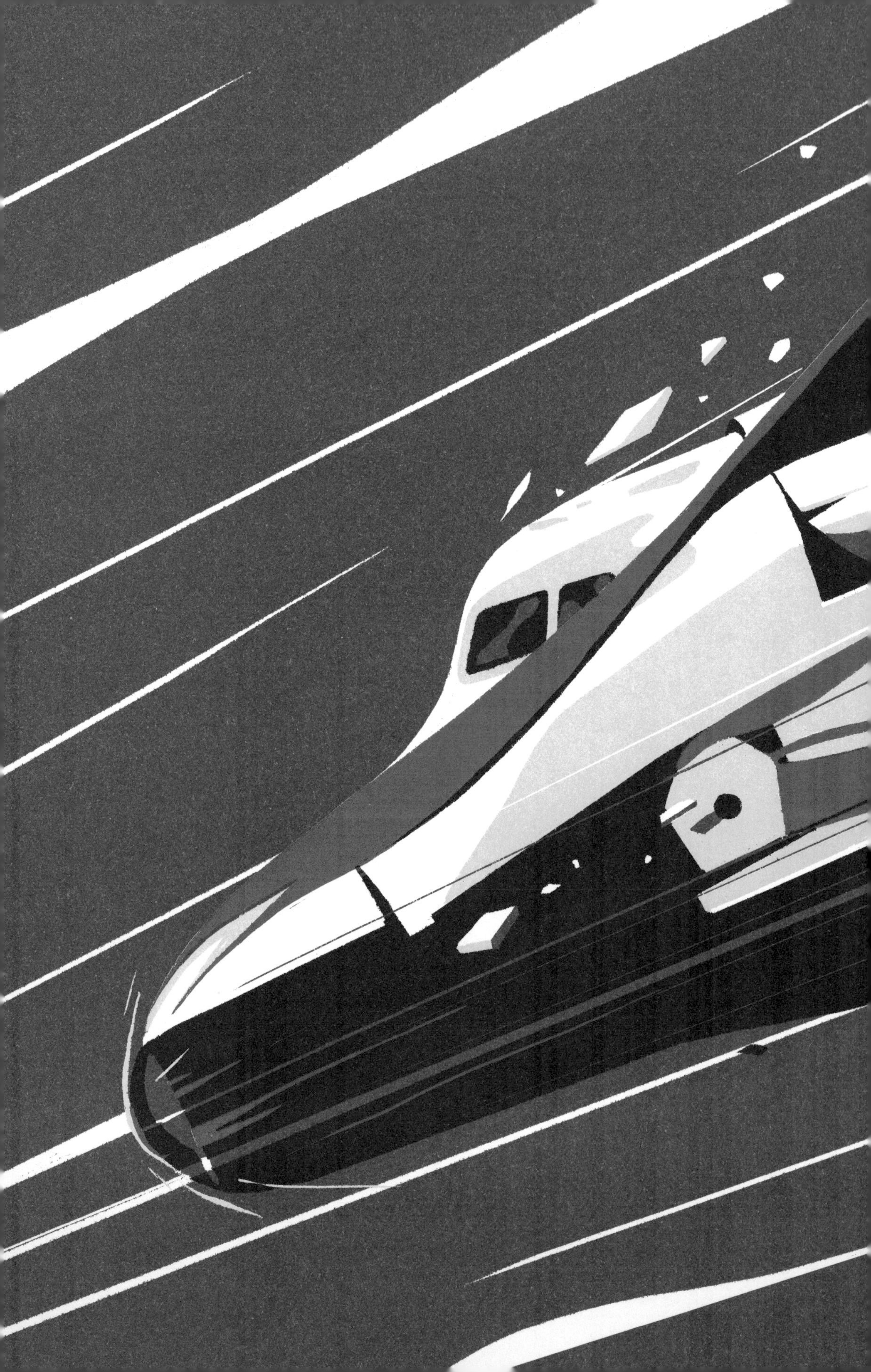

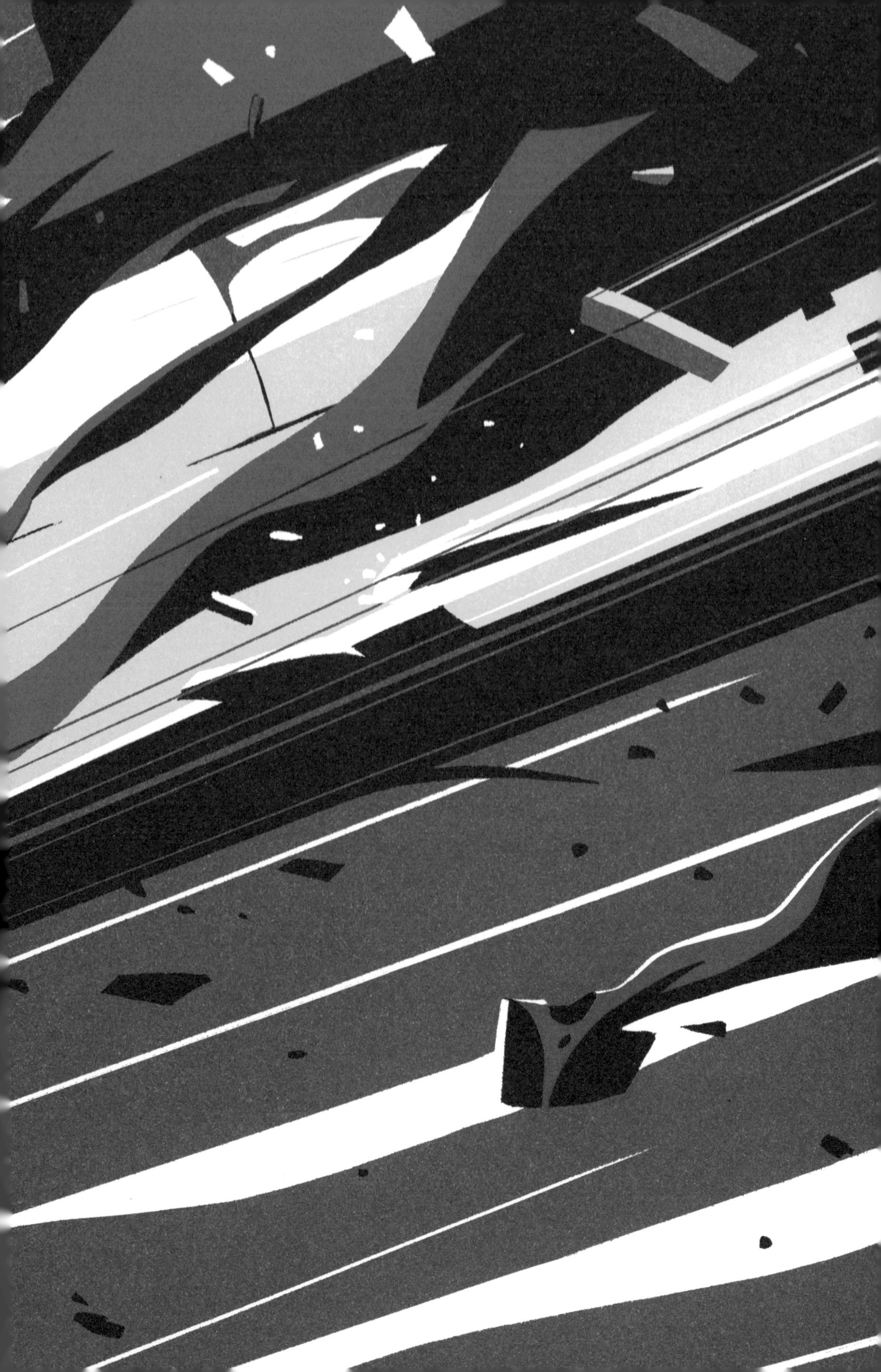

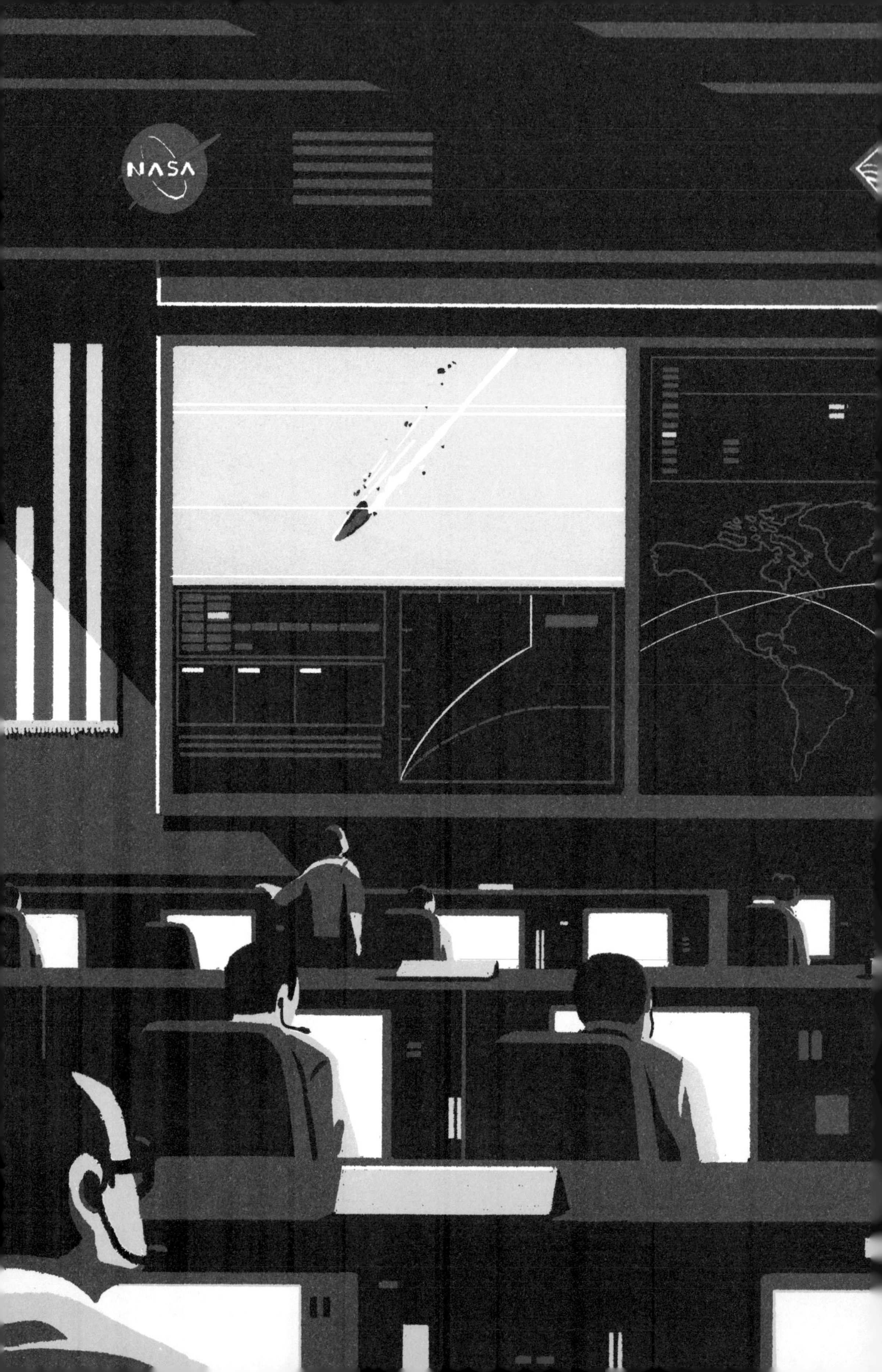
NASA

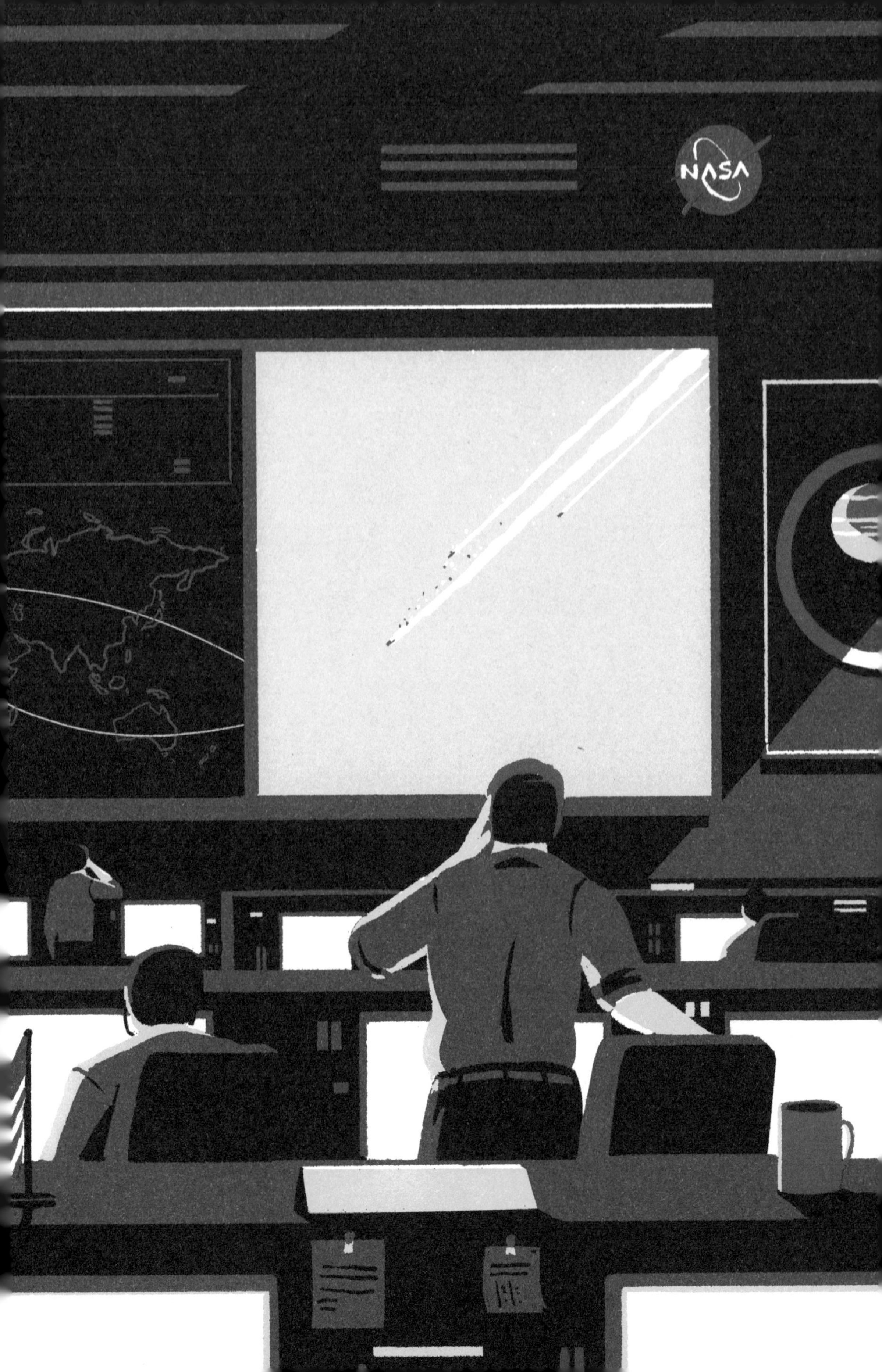
NASA

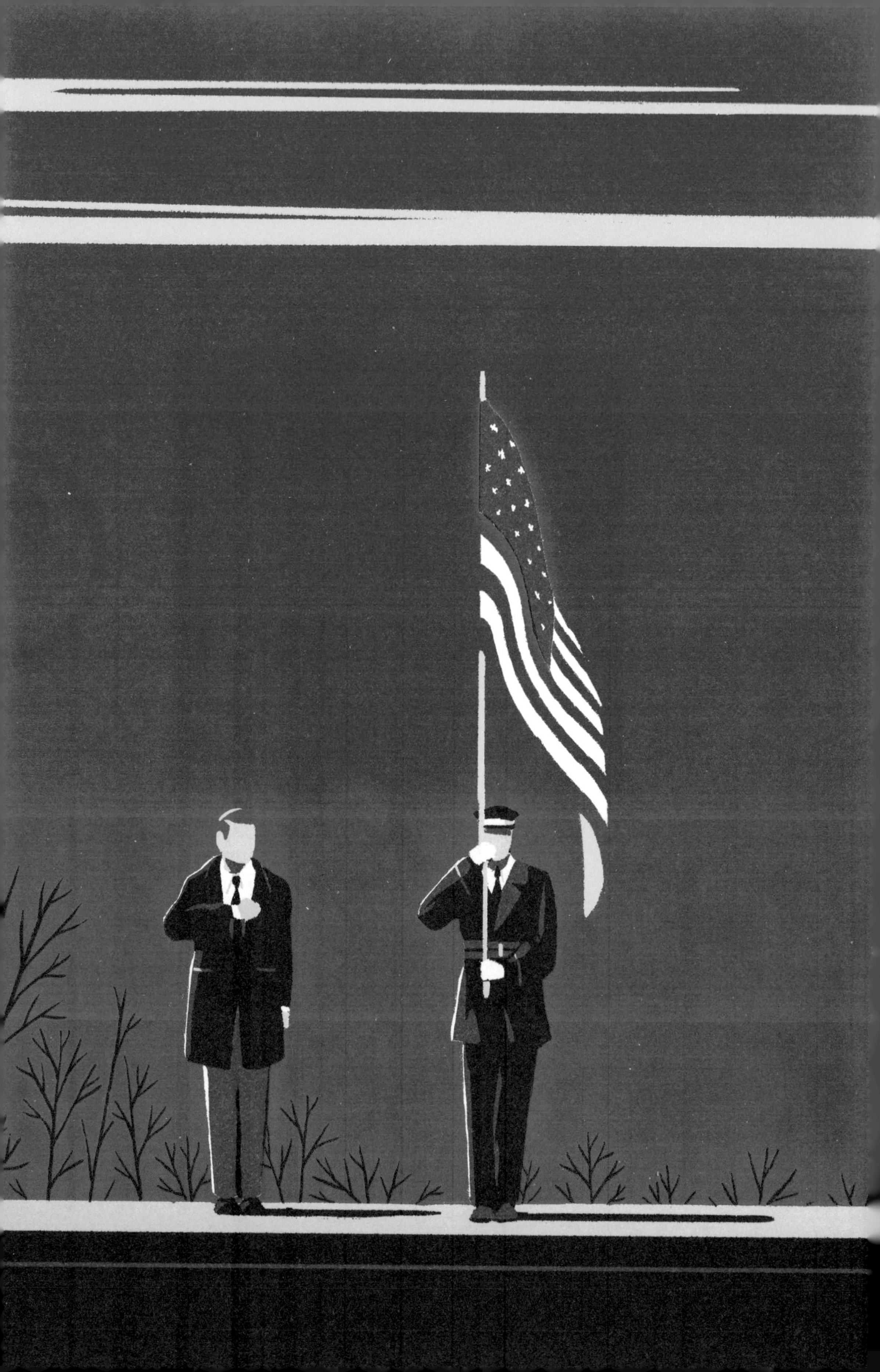

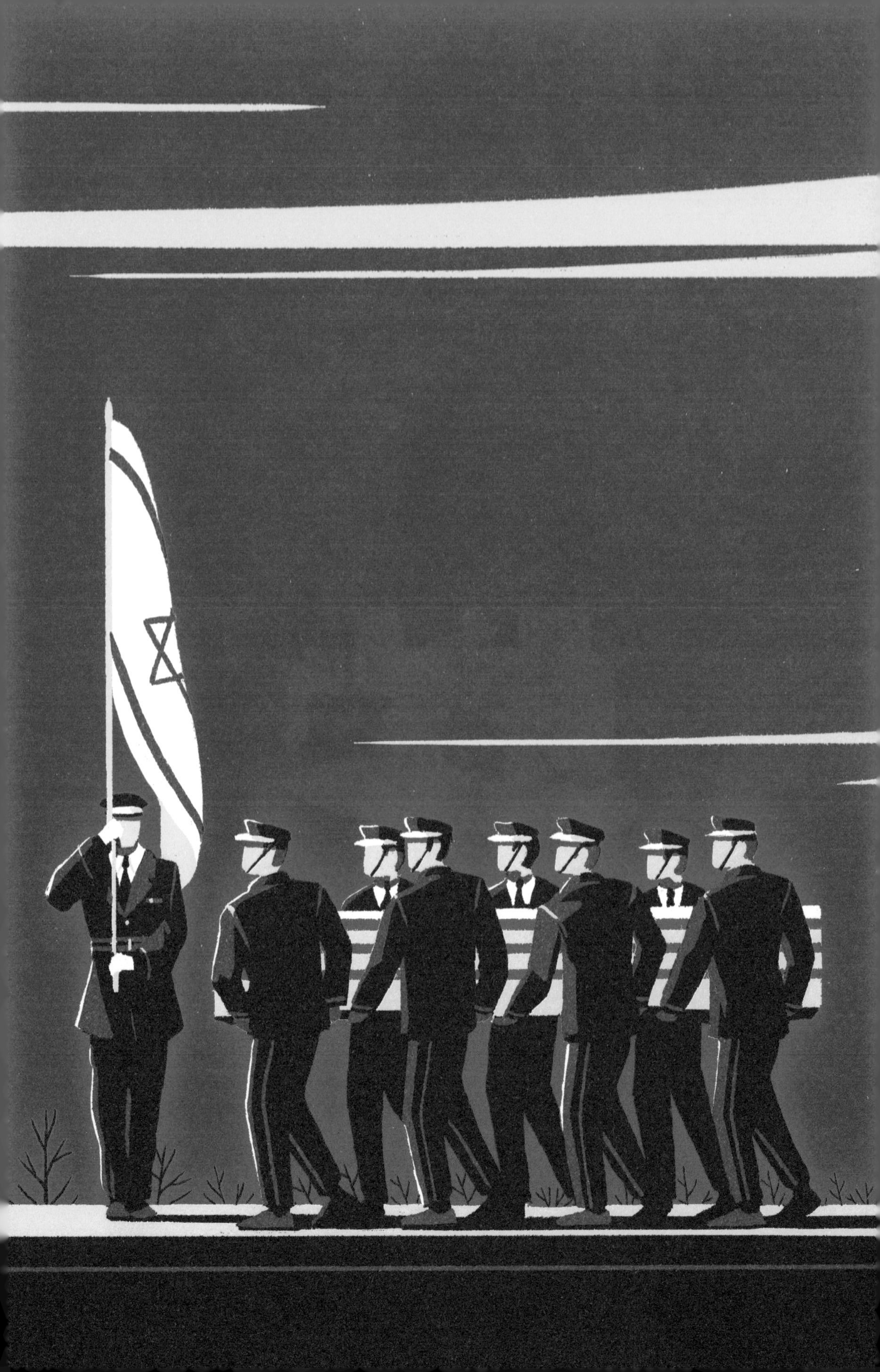

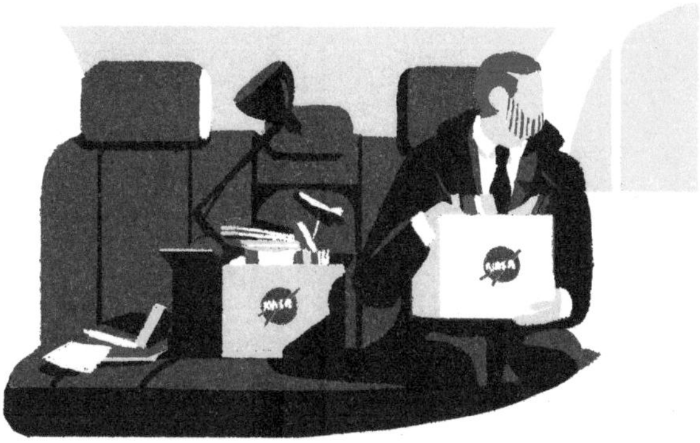
NASA
NASA

FEBRUARY 2004,
JOHNSON SPACE CENTER, HOUSTON, TEXAS

NASA

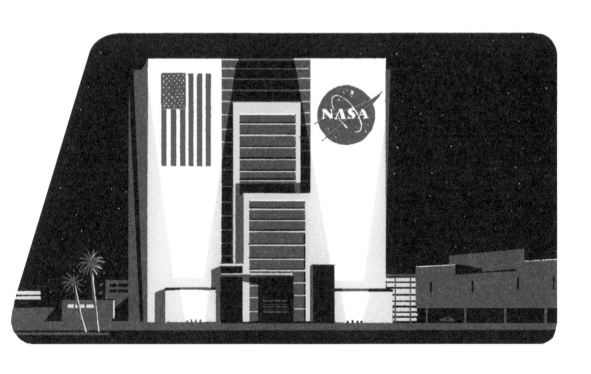

APRIL 2005,
CAPITOL STREET, HOUSTON, TEXAS

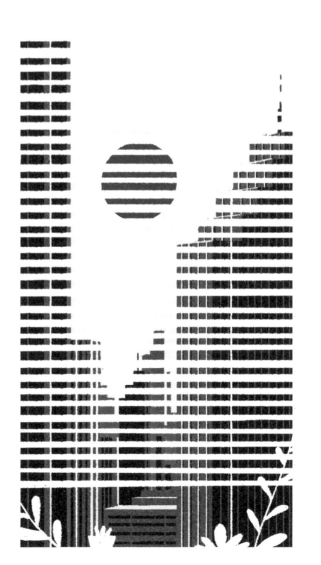

JUNE 2006,
CAPITOL STREET, HOUSTON, TEXAS

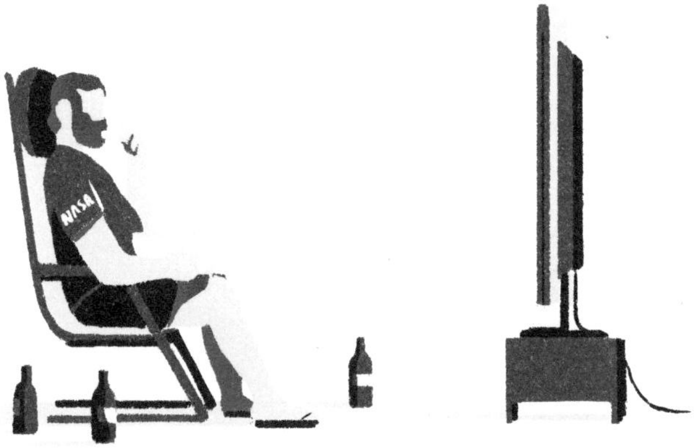
NASA

JANUARY 2007,
CAPITOL STREET, HOUSTON, TEXAS

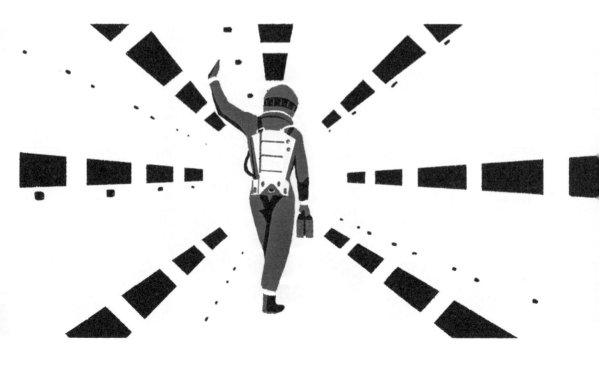

JUNE 2008,
RIVER OAKS, HOUSTON, TEXAS

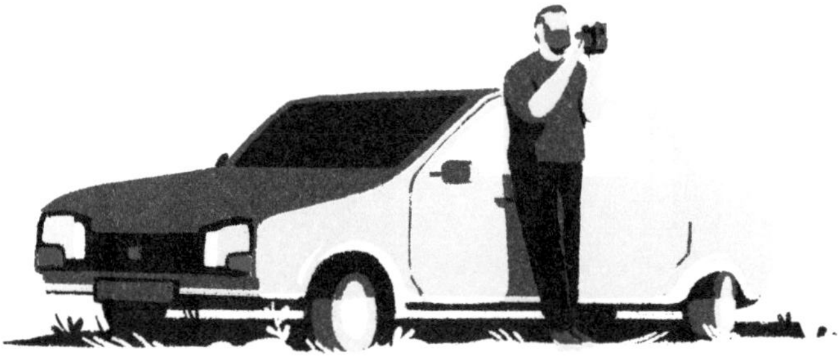

MAY 2009,

SHUTTLE DISCOVERY, KENNEDY SPACE CENTER, CAPE CANAVERAL, FLORIDA

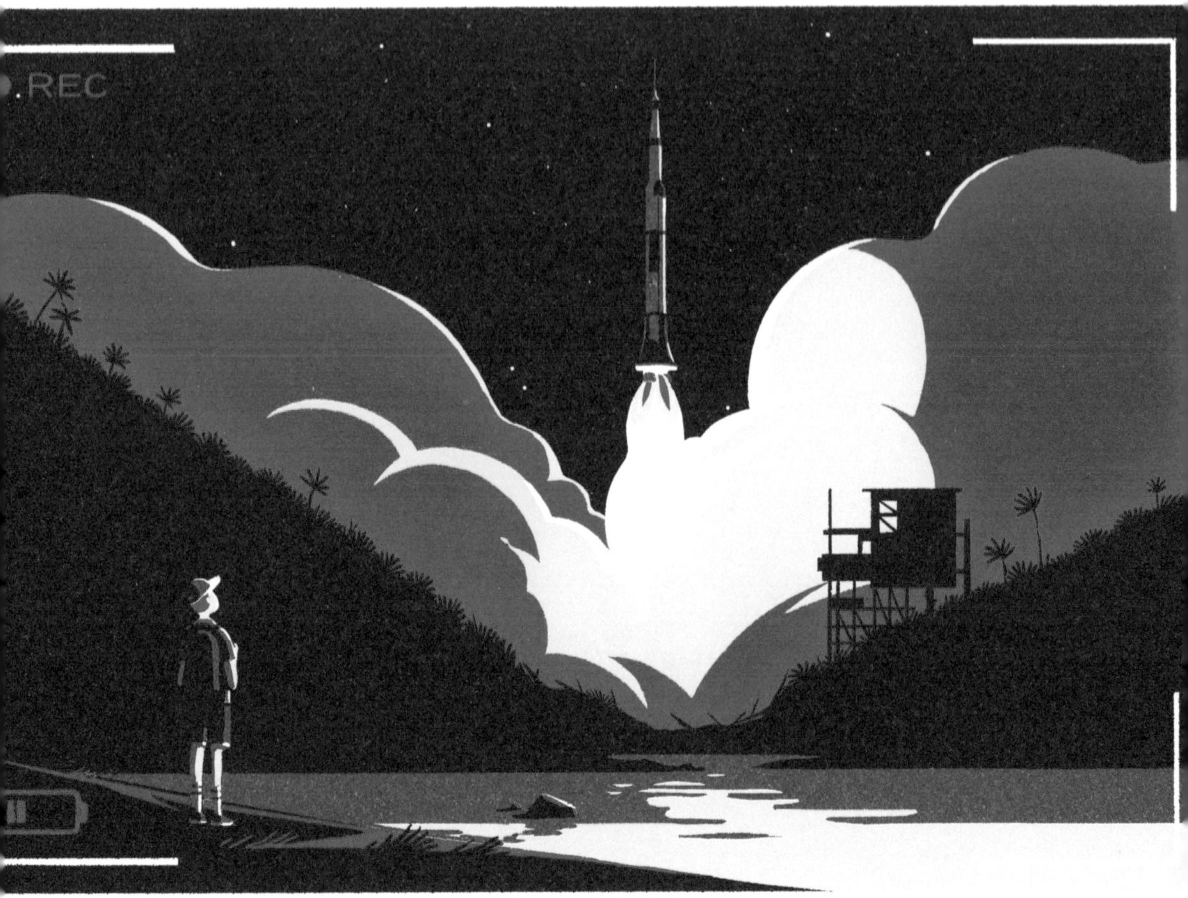

REC

DECEMBER 2010,
GEORGE BUSH INTERCONTINENTAL AIRPORT, HOUSTON, TEXAS

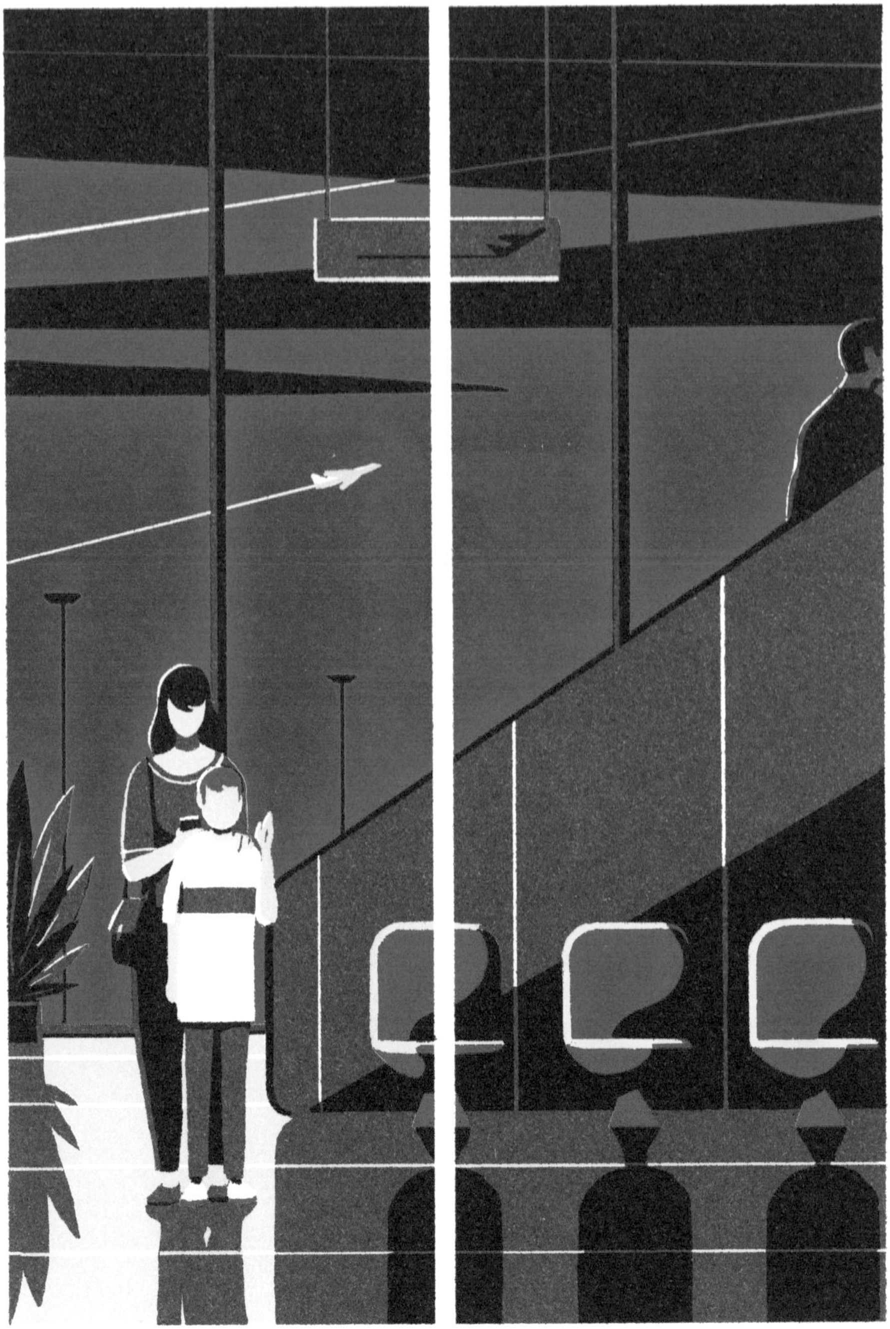

JANUARY 2011,
MUD BAY, KETCHIKAN, ALASKA

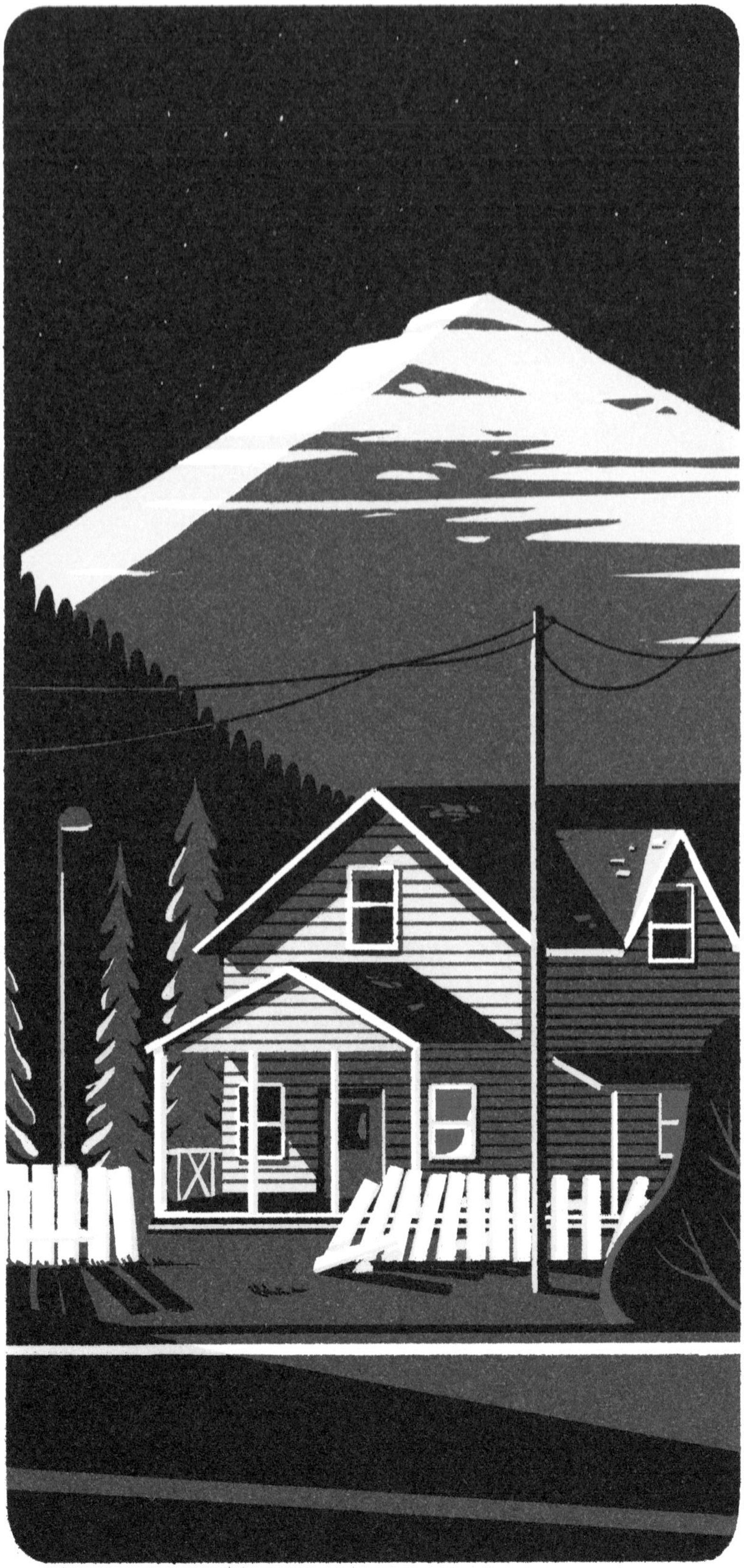

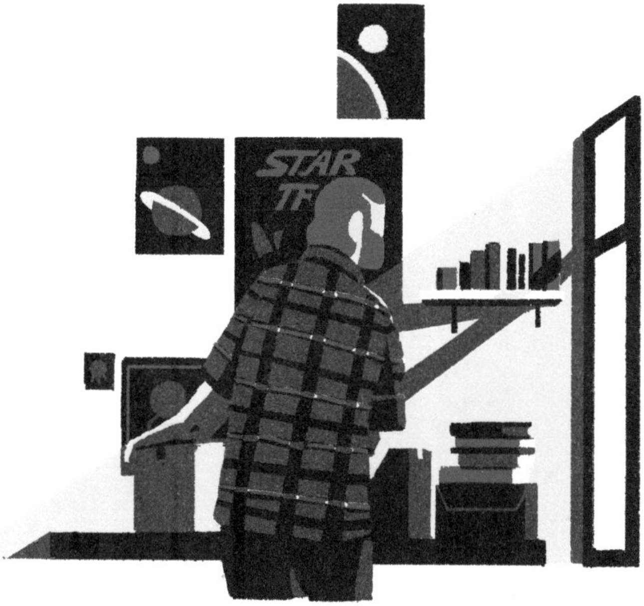
STAR
TF

JUNE 2012,
MUD BAY, KETCHIKAN, ALASKA

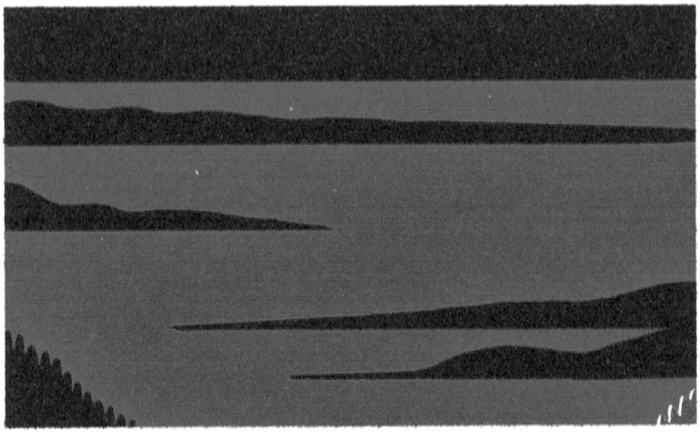

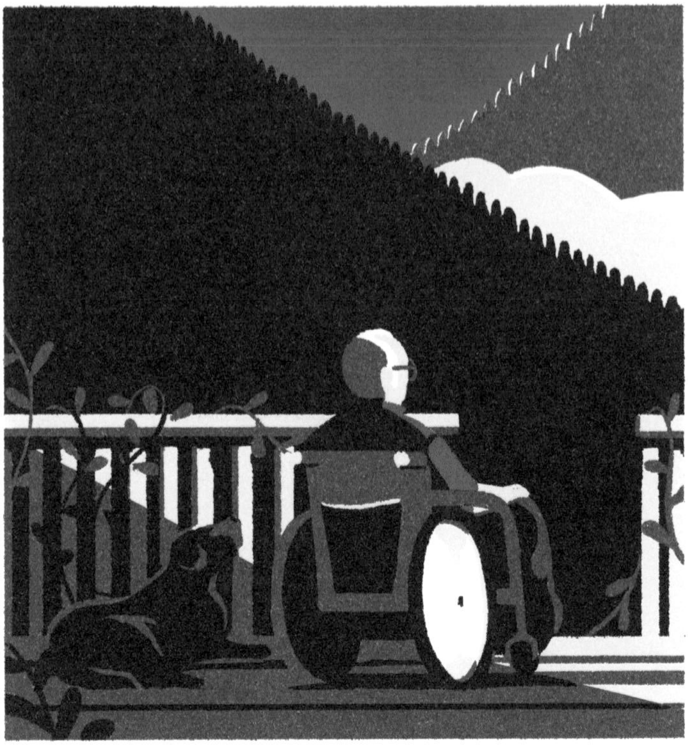

APRIL 2013,
MUD BAY, KETCHIKAN, ALASKA

NOVEMBER 2014,
PENNOCK ISLAND, KETCHIKAN, ALASKA

APRIL 2015,
GRAVINA ISLAND CHURCH, KETCHIKAN, ALASKA

OCTOBER 2016,
MUD BAY, KETCHIKAN, ALASKA

JUNE 2017,
PENNOCK ISLAND, KETCHIKAN, ALASKA

OCTOBER 2018,
MUD BAY, KETCHIKAN, ALASKA

MAY 2019,
MUD BAY, KETCHIKAN, ALASKA

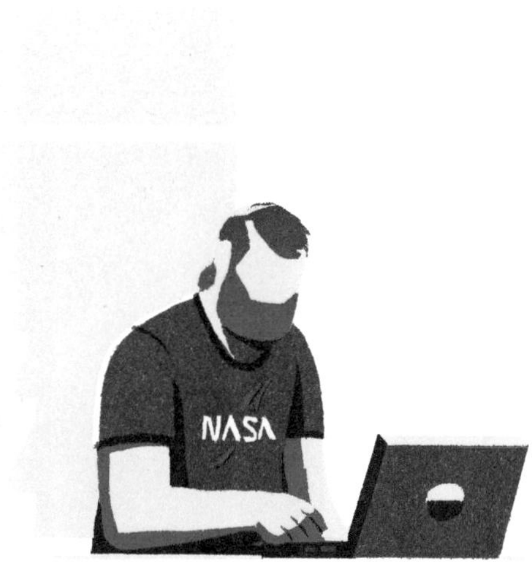
NASA

SEPTEMBER 2020,
MUD BAY, KETCHIKAN, ALASKA

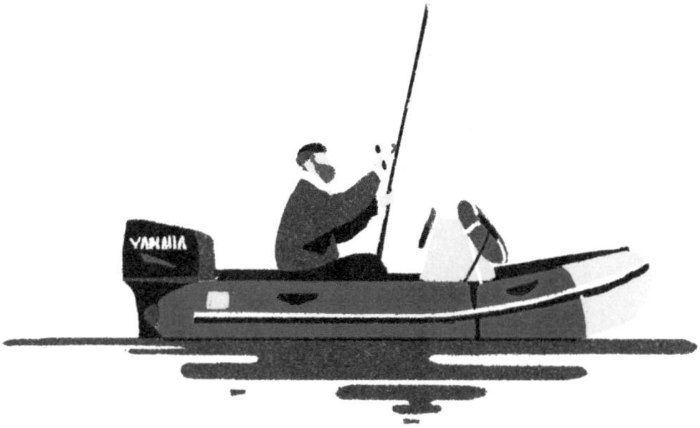
YAMAHA

APRIL 2021,
WHITMAN LAKE, KETCHIKAN, ALASKA

JULY 2022,
MUD BAY, KETCHIKAN, ALASKA

NOVEMBER 2023,
MUD BAY, KETCHIKAN, ALASKA

OCTOBER 2024,
MUD BAY, KETCHIKAN, ALASKA

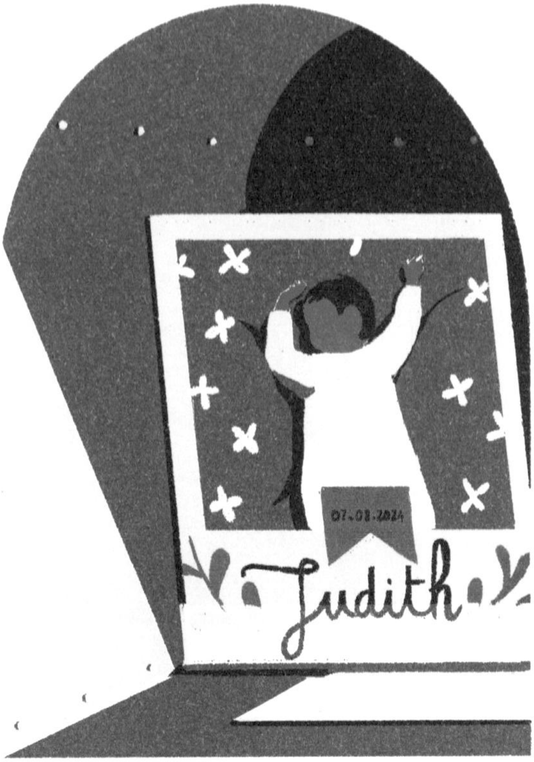
07.08.2024
Judith

DECEMBER 2025,
MUD BAY, KETCHIKAN, ALASKA

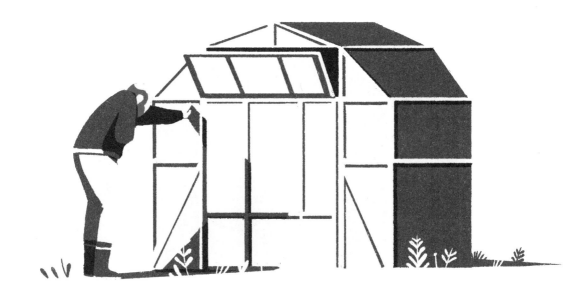

APRIL 2026,
MUD BAY, KETCHIKAN, ALASKA

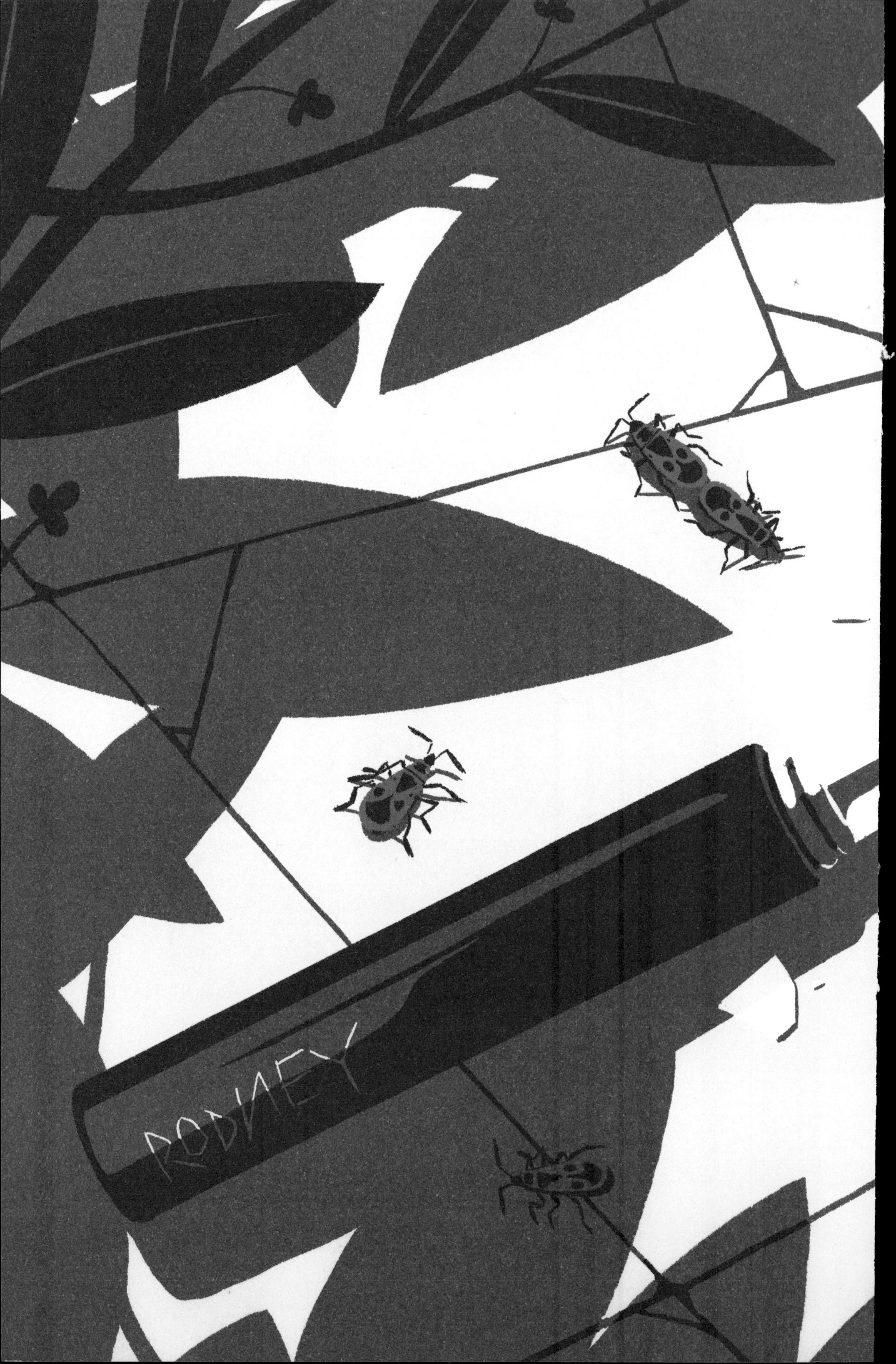
RODNEY

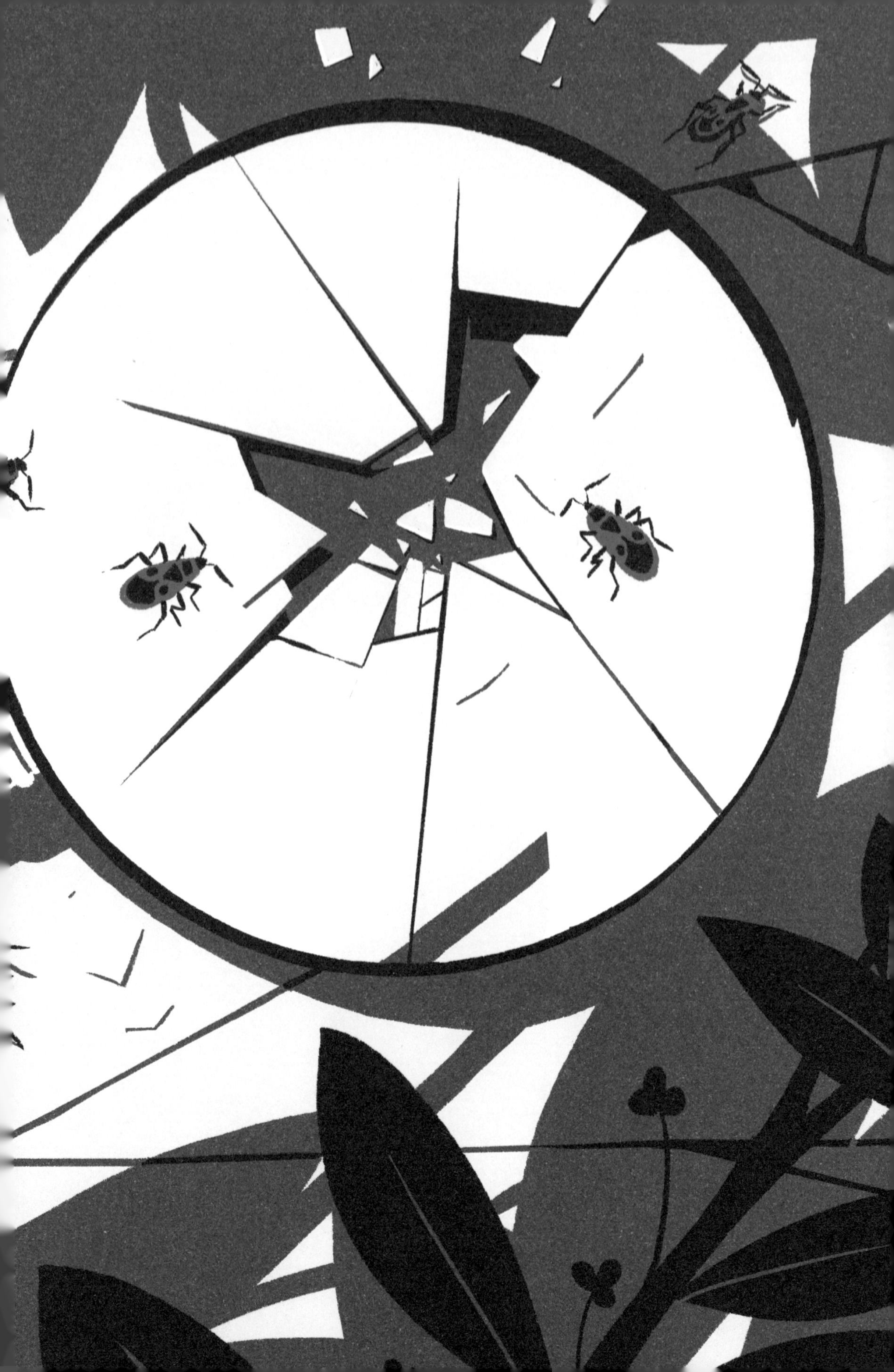

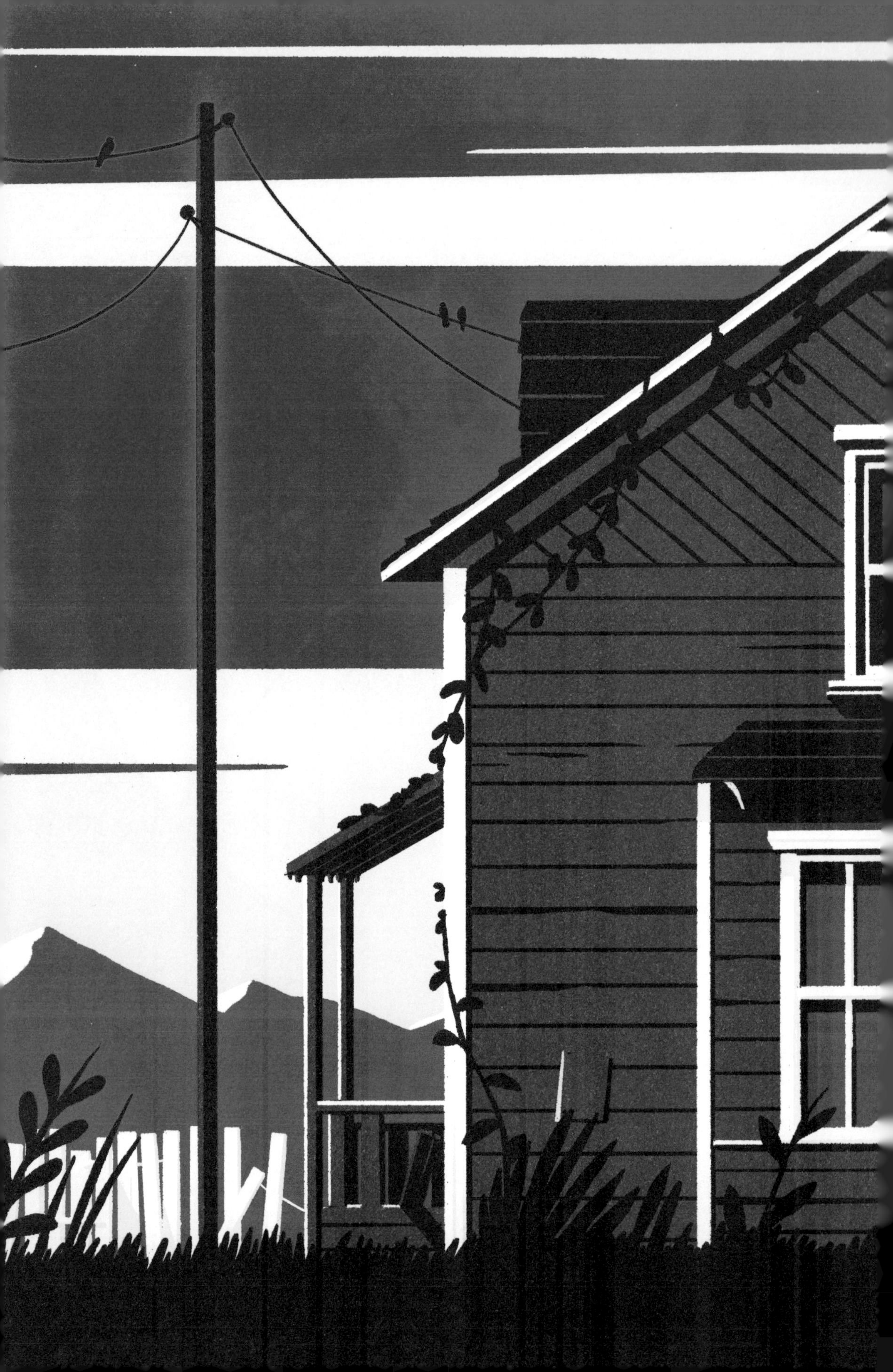

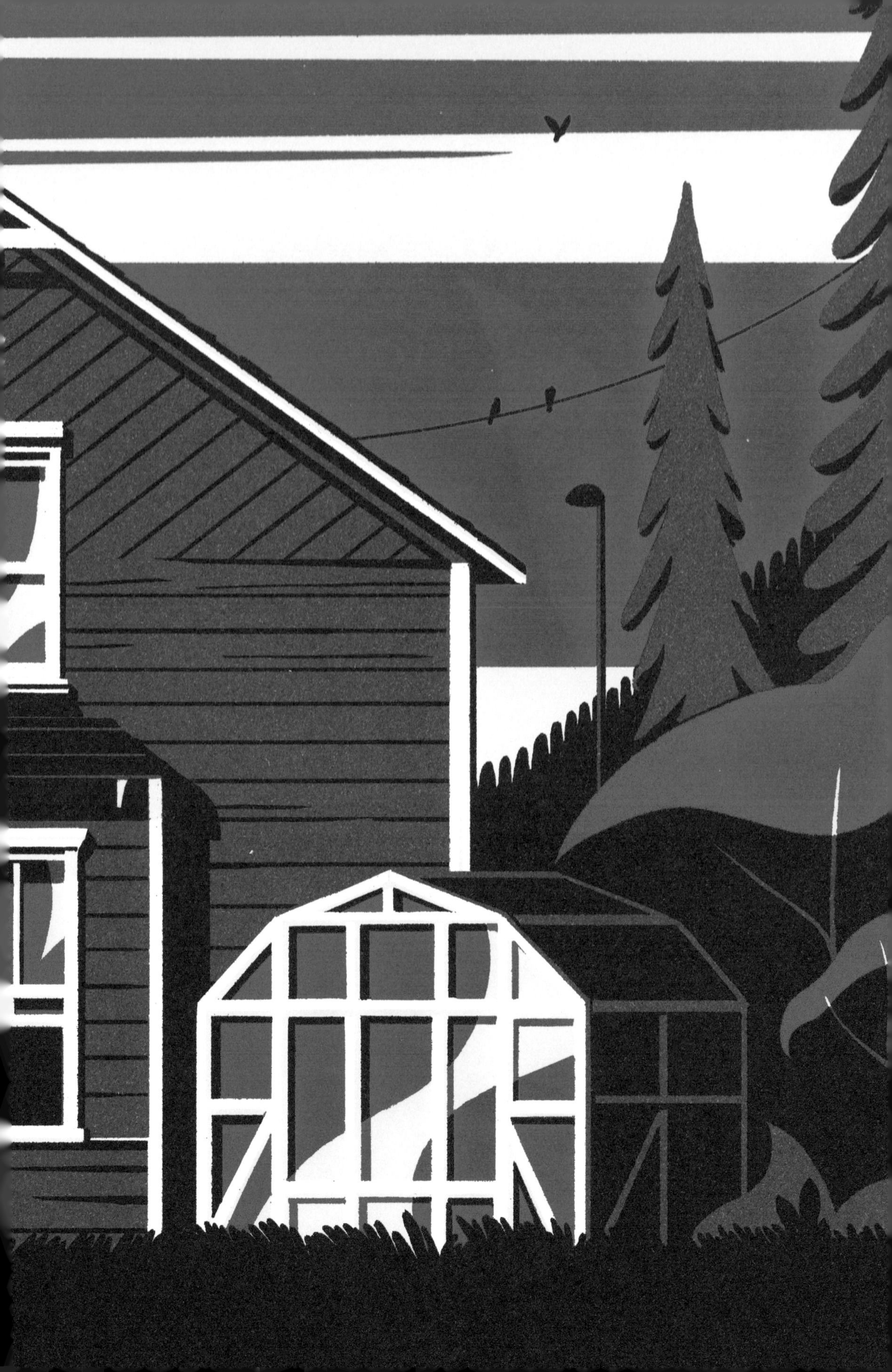

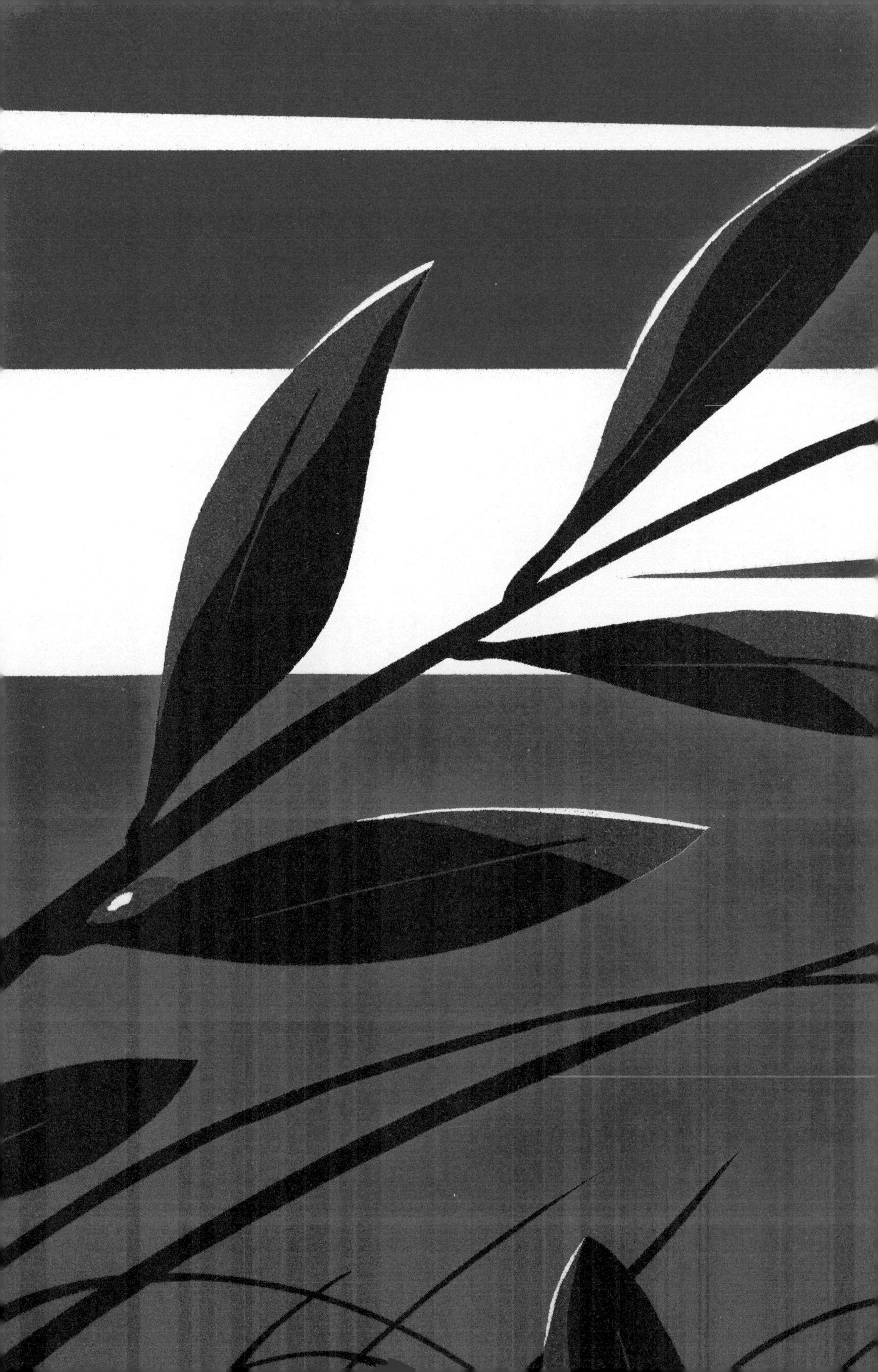

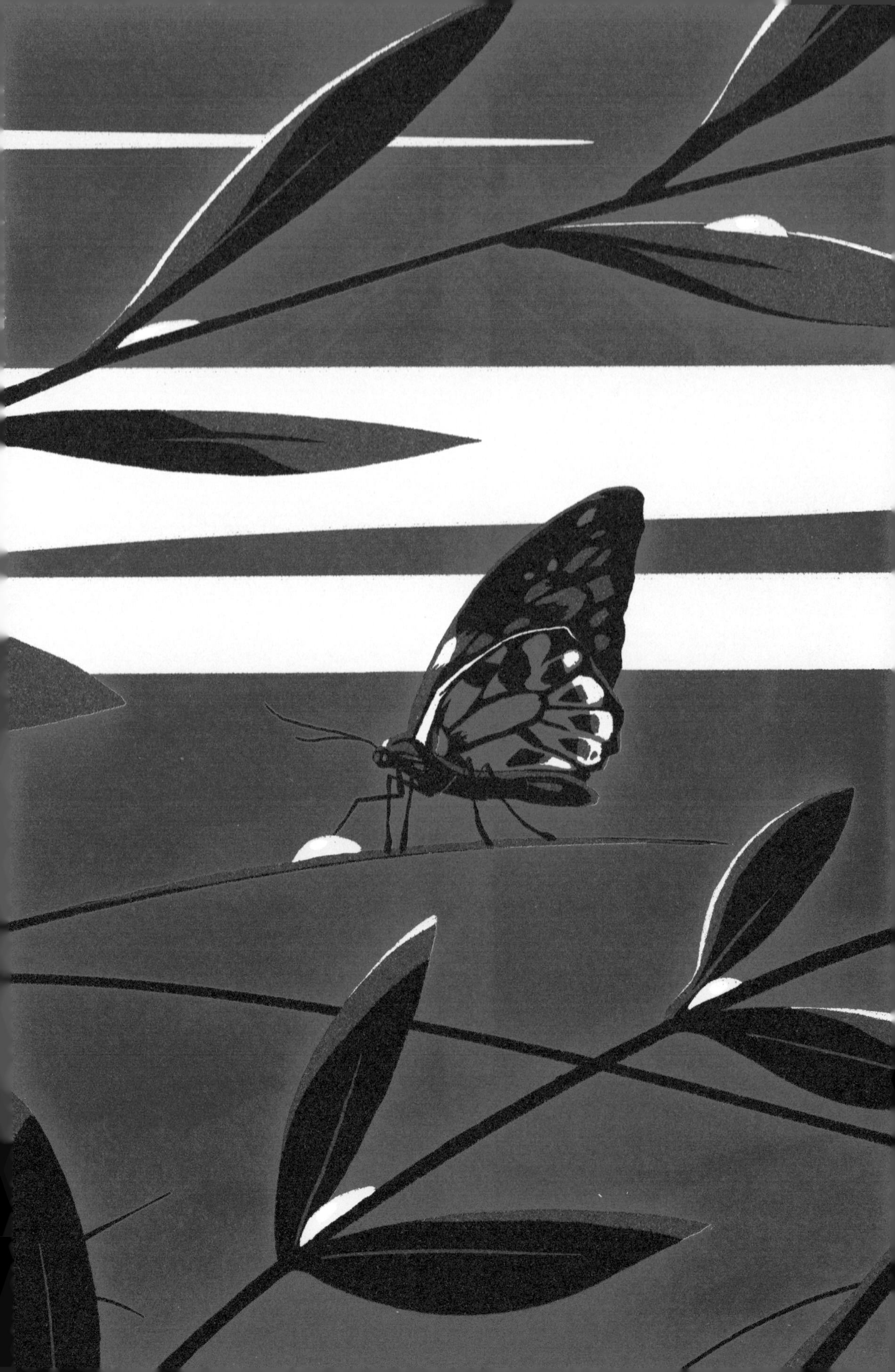

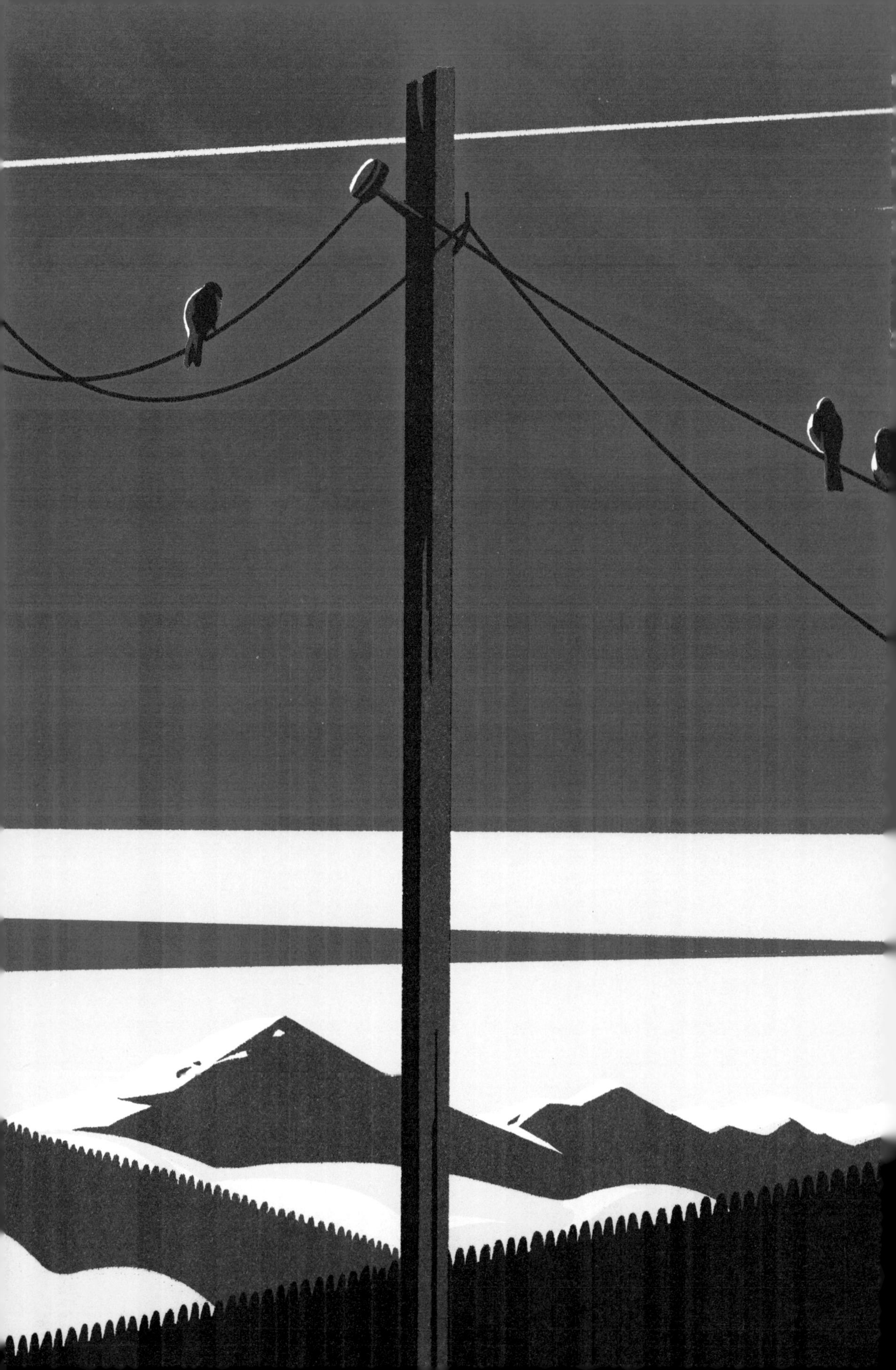

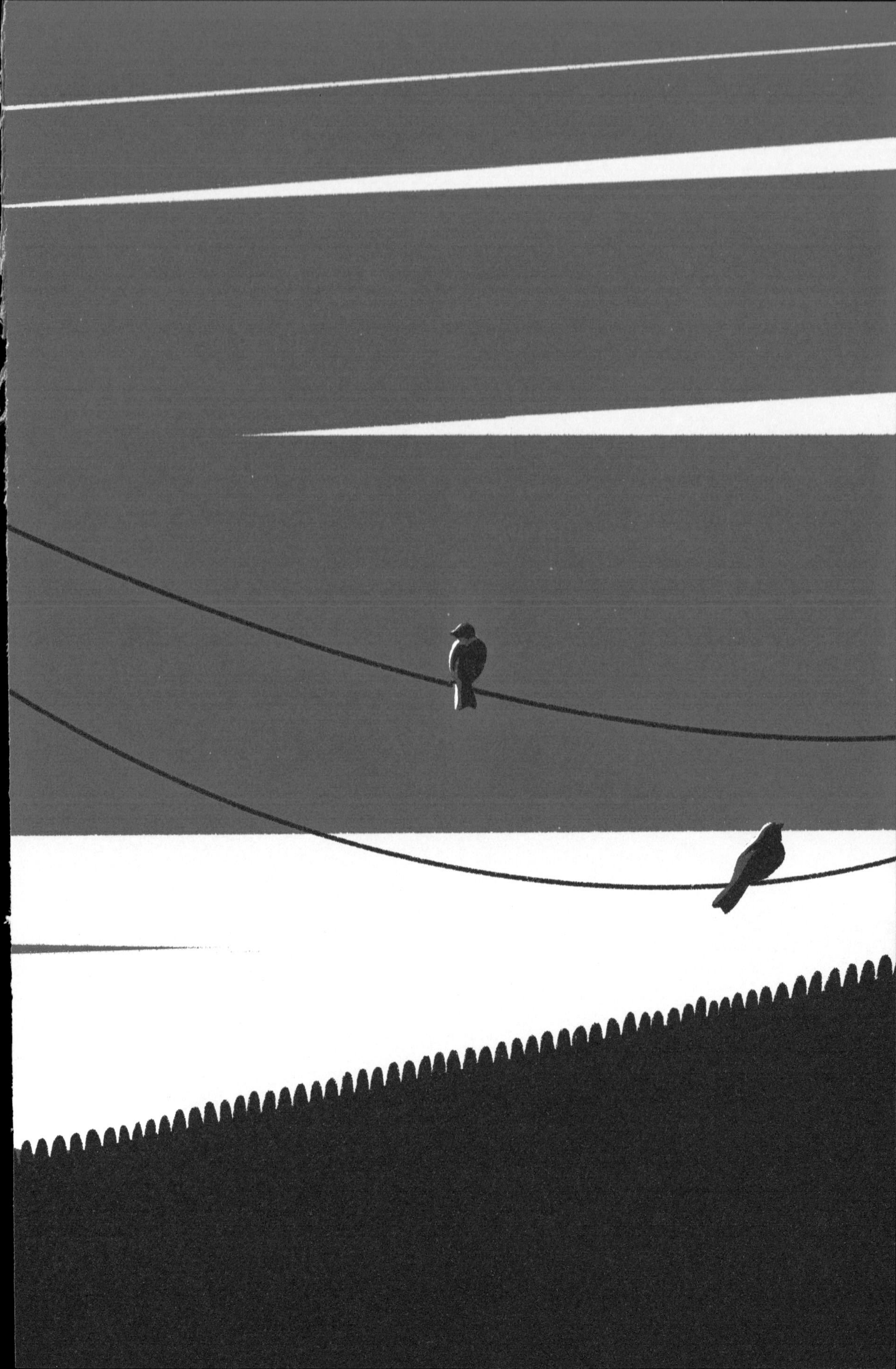

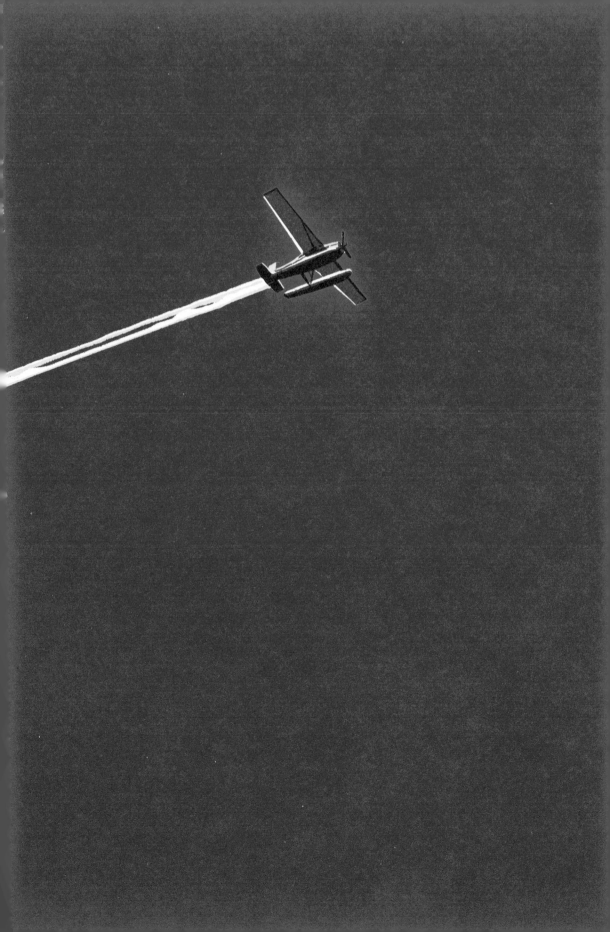